Gary & Nuala's GUIDE TO LAS VEGAS and beyond

GARY ARCHER | NUALA O'BRIEN

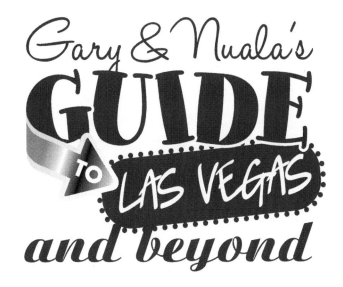

MEMOIRS
Cirencester

Published by Memoirs

MEMOIRS
PUBLISHING

Memoirs Books

25 Market Place, Cirencester, Gloucestershire, GL7 2NX
info@memoirsbooks.co.uk   www.memoirspublishing.com

Copyright © Gary Archer, April 2012
First published in England, 2012

ISBN 978-1-909020-28-3

Printed in England

CONTENTS

Foreword
About this book

Foreword

People have been asking us questions for years about Las Vegas and the USA in general, as we have travelled so extensively around it. Some of the questions we get asked most often are - how much money should we take? What's the weather like? How much will it cost? (Most people think the States is more expensive to visit than it actually is, as long as you're reasonably frugal).

Having been to the area countless times, we know it very well, so we don't mind answering people's questions and putting their concerns to rest. It's nice to be helpful, especially when you know about the subject in hand.

Several people have gone on to ask us why we don't write a book about Las Vegas. For a long time we didn't really take this suggestion seriously. And then one day we were in a restaurant in Vegas and overheard two waitresses discussing the impending opening of the new Hoover Dam Memorial bridge. They had no idea that the bridge had already been open for a while. That was the point at which we realised that we know more about the area than some of the locals – and made the decision that it was time to write that book our friends had been asking for.

We hope you enjoy reading it as much as we enjoyed writing it.

About this book

Everyone knows what Las Vegas is famous for – the gambling, the lights and the night-life. This book has been written to show visitors to the area just how much more the area has to offer, if you venture outside the city limits and out into the wider world of the Las Vegas Valley and beyond.

Some of the most spectacular sights the USA has to offer can be found within a day's drive of Vegas. You can tour the stunning rock formations of Utah, see the Grand Canyon and the Arizona Meteor Crater and view the stunning Hoover Dam, to name a few.

Wherever you're travelling from, you can use this guide to make sure your holiday in the Las Vegas area is memorable, for all the right reasons. It just takes some inside knowledge and a little planning. This book will supply the first – it's up to you to do the rest.

If this is going to be your first visit, then you may not want to go too far, as you will probably be exploring the Strip (the main resort area of Las Vegas) and taking a few day trips to see the main sights of the region, such as the Hoover Dam and the Grand Canyon. More about them later on.

If you've been to the area before, then maybe you're aiming to see a little less of the bright lights and the noisy casinos and a little more of the fascinating states of Nevada, Arizona, Utah and California.

Everything you'll read in these pages has been gathered from personal experience over 15 years of visits to the Las Vegas area. Every photograph has been taken by us, and all the illustrations and maps are our own work. We have tried to present the material as simply and clearly as possible.

You'll come across many national and state parks when travelling around, and you will need to pay a fee almost every time you enter one. The book lists how much each park costs to enter (please bear in mind that fees may be increased at any time). The most expensive we have come across so far has been the Grand Canyon National Park at $25 per vehicle, but for the most part they range between $5 and $15. For motorcycles, cyclists and pedestrians the fees are less.

Some of the places mentioned are too far from the city to be visited without an overnight stay, so in these cases we suggest you buy yourself a road map and make yourself familiar with your route before you set off. Road names and numbers are of course given in the book, along with anything else that will make finding your destination easier.

I have stated the approximate distance in miles at the start of each section. The mileage is from the centre of the Strip in Las Vegas and is one way only.

If you are travelling from the UK, you will need to use the ESTA (Electronic System for Travel Authorisation). I have given details of how this works.

There is information about hotels and any hidden charges you may not know about at the time of booking, such as resort fees.

I have explained how to get the best deals on flights, and if you are planning to hire a car and have never driven in the USA before there is some useful guidance here as well, to help make your driving experience easier and more enjoyable.

Booking

So you're sitting at home thinking about getting some sunshine and seeing the sights of Las Vegas, but you don't really know where to start, which website to look at or which travel agent to call. Are you going to pay too much? Where are the best deals? Which airline should you use? How much money should you take? Where do you rent a car? All these questions can seem very daunting - I know, I have been there.

The information in these pages is based on our experience visiting America from the UK. If you live elsewhere you will naturally need to find out what the procedure is for entering the States from your country, although the booking procedure will be basically the same anywhere in the world.

Of course, you may decide to simply go to the high street or call a travel agent or tour operator and let them do all the hard work for you. All you do is hand over the money. If that's what you prefer, rather than having the hassle of searching lots of websites and hunting down the best deals, that's fine - there is lots more information throughout this book that will help you to enjoy your trip.

However, we think there is great satisfaction to be had from booking it all yourself and knowing you have obtained the best deals. You can save a lot of money and explore more options by planning your own holiday. And after you have done it once, it will be much easier the second and third time.

Some people have said to me that they don't feel confident enough to book everything themselves and they are afraid something may go wrong. They may forget something important, get the dates wrong or get ripped off and pay too much. Well yes, this could happen, so you have to have your wits about you and make sure you double-check everything.

You may fear you have no protection if something goes wrong

unless you book the whole holiday through a travel agent or a recognised internet travel company. Yet what happens if the company goes bust? You will have all your eggs in one basket so to speak. They may be covered by the industry regulators, but that may not stop you losing your holiday - and how long will you have to wait to get your money back? If you do get it back.

There are some precautions you should take. Find out when you book the flight if the ticket is going to be refundable or not. Airlines have different rules, so it's always worth reading the small print. Of course if you buy a flexible ticket this can be refunded and even have the dates changed, but this will almost always cost you more at the time of booking.

If you cancel in reasonable time, you should normally expect a full refund,   though hotels sometimes charge a small administration fee. Once when we booked two weeks' car hire and decided to cancel, the money was fully refunded with no charges, as we cancelled more than 48 hours before collection. This was only possible because we had decided not to rush into hiring a car from the first day – we've learned it's best to spend two or three days soaking up the sun and chilling out before we pick up the car, so there was plenty of time to cancel and get a full refund. More about car rental later.

The airport in Vegas is very close to the strip and the hotels, so getting to a hotel is very easy. Not that we're suggesting you walk – Vegas can be seriously hot in summer.

Some hotels run a free shuttle bus for their guests, and for others there are shuttle buses running around the clock to take you to almost all the hotels for a fee of around $7 per person. If there are more than two of you, a taxi may work out cheaper. There are always plenty of taxis at the airport and around Vegas.

I can only advise you of the way we think is best and the way we like to book our trips, via the Internet. It does take a bit of surfing, so you need to set aside a morning, afternoon or evening. We do it this way because we like to stay where we want to stay and not at a hotel that comes with a certain package. We like to put together our own little package, which will contain everything we want. We choose the flight we want, the hotel and car that suit us and all the excursions and trips that interest us.

To us there's nothing worse than having to be somewhere at a certain time to catch a coach to go on a trip. Then when you arrive, no sooner do you find something you want to spend time investigating than it's time to catch the coach back! No thank you, that's not for us. OK enough of that for now, let's get started.

GETTING INTO THE USA

ESTA (Electronic System for Travel Authorisation)

Before attempting to travel to the USA you must check to see if your country participates in the American Visa Waiver Program. The best way to do this is to get online and check with the American Embassy web page. I am a British citizen and I know that the United Kingdom has participated in the program for many years. So do 29 other European countries, as well as Australia and New Zealand and certain Asian countries.

If your country participates, there is one thing you MUST do before you book anything, and that's apply for an ESTA, (Electronic System for Travel Authorisation).

Oh my God, what's that? I hear you ask - well don't panic, it's no big deal. It's just an online form you have to complete before being allowed to enter the USA. If your country does not participate, then this section will not apply to you, and you should make arrangements to apply for a visa.

ESTA is a web-based system that will tell you in advance if you are eligible to travel to the USA under the Visa Waiver Program. The ESTA system now replaces the green visa waiver forms we all had to complete on the plane in the old days, with no guarantee you would be accepted on arrival. The blue and white form that asks what goods and moneys we are taking into the country still has to be completed on the plane. There still is no guarantee that you will be allowed into the USA – that decision is made by the US customs officer who stamps your passport at the point of entry. The ESTA system just establishes ahead of time if you are 'eligible to travel'. But it is useful to be able to find out before booking if we are going to be allowed entry.

This may sound very scary, but don't panic - there are very few horror stories of people being denied entry. Unless you have failed to declare a criminal record or something else that may hinder your entry, in which case it will of course be your own fault.

I cannot stress enough how important this is. If you do not complete the ESTA you will NOT be allowed into the USA - you will be turned back.

Everyone going to the USA under the visa waiver program, by air or sea, must fill out an ESTA, even if you are just passing through on your way to another destination outside the USA. It has to be done in advance and can only be done online. So if for any reason you do not have the internet at home you will have to go to a friend's house or the library.

The process takes only a few minutes, and tells you at the end if you have been accepted or not.

Initially the ESTA programme was free, but a charge of $14 has now been introduced. Some of this money is said to be allocated to promoting tourism in the USA, though charging people an entry fee to visit the country they are trying to promote doesn't seem the best way to do it!

The website you need to visit to complete your ESTA is that of the US Department of Homeland Security at DHS.GOV (Department of Homeland Security). On the 'immigration' tab click 'visiting the USA', then click on ESTA.

This is the official US homeland security website and the only website you should use to complete your ESTA. If you search for ESTA on the web you will come across many websites offering to help you complete your ESTA application, but these sites will charge you a much higher fee and you really don't need any help as it's fairly basic information you need to provide.

So remember, the only fee you need to pay is to the US homeland security website.

It's worth noting that if for some reason you fail in your ESTA application there is still a $4 administration fee to pay, but it's a small price compared to the inconvenience if you had booked everything else first.

When completing the ESTA you may notice it asks for the address of the hotel you will be staying at and the flight number you will be arriving on. But you haven't booked these yet, so enter any Las Vegas hotel and flight number for now, and when you have booked you can come back and update this information.

The good news is that once you have completed the ESTA it is valid for two years. All you have to do the next time you travel to the USA is update the location where you will be staying and the flight number you are entering the country on. This is easy and only takes a few minutes. If you are moving around, or staying in different locations during your visit, you need only put down the address of the hotel you are staying at for the first night, or the address if you are visiting friends.

When you do your first ESTA make sure you print off a copy or make a note of the application number, as you will need this number to retrieve your ESTA from the homeland security website when you want to update any information. If for any reason you can't find the number or you cannot retrieve your ESTA, you will need to complete a new application and pay another $14 fee.

When going through customs after arriving in the USA you will not be asked to produce your ESTA, because the customs officer will already know if you have completed one or not. In fact they won't even mention anything about your ESTA, unless you neglected to do one of course, and then it will certainly be the main topic of conversation.

We always take our printed copy's with us just in case there is any complication with their computer system, so we can produce it if needed. This has never happened yet but we will always take a copy, just in case!

Flights and booking

Once you have been approved to enter the USA, you need to book the flight. I always think that if the flight is booked first you can get a hotel in Las Vegas, or anywhere else, to match the flight dates. If the hotel is booked first it is much more difficult to get flights to match the dates you have booked at the hotel, and if you do find one it may be much more expensive. So book the flight first.

There are several sites you should search besides those of the airline companies. It just depends when you search which will be cheaper.

Sometimes we have found a reasonable flight with one of the well-known internet travel sites, but then we have found the same flight cheaper by going direct to the airline's website. Sometimes it can happen the other way around, so as I say, it all depends when you search.

We have generally found there is no good time to search. If you can't find the flight you want, turn off the computer and come back to it later on or the following day – you'll find the right flight for the right price in the end. But mostly we get lucky first or second time.

Most UK flights to Las Vegas leave England in the morning, from Heathrow or Gatwick. I can't speak for other airports such as Manchester as we have never flown from there, but you can easily find out. There are only so many flights to the USA on any one day, so the airlines and the flight times will soon become familiar after a short time searching. This goes for other European countries too, so make yourself familiar with the flight times from your chosen airport.

Surfing for flights

Now get yourself on to some travel websites. There are plenty to choose from, so take your time. Try the airlines' websites and search all these too. You may want to do an internet search to start with, to see which airlines fly to the USA, as you don't really want to spend time putting information into airline websites if they only fly to Europe. You will also find a list of airlines which fly to the USA at the back of this book.

If you prefer a direct flight to Las Vegas, there are several to choose from. It will nearly always cost you more, but if you don't mind paying the extra then go for it. It is always a good idea to check those websites anyway, as in the past we have found some very good deals on direct flights. Again, it depends when you look!

Generally you will be booking a flight with one stop going and one stop coming home, normally in the same place. I don't mean a stop in another country, this stop will always be in the USA - for example, Philadelphia or Chicago. When you have found the flight you want, it is just a matter of finding the cheapest place to book it.

Finally, when you're happy with all the details, you click the button to pay and the website displays the page that says, 'Thank you, your flight is confirmed'. This is when we start grinning from ear to ear, as this is the point at which we know we are really going and when. Everything else can now be planned and booked around the flights.

For the purpose of this book let's assume you are taking a flight to Las Vegas from Heathrow and stopping in Chicago on the way. Chicago is where you will clear US Customs, so be prepared for a bit of a wait if several flights have come in at once. This is not always the case, sometimes we just glide through customs with no queuing at all. But you always clear customs at the first place you land in the USA. This is where they will decide if they are going to let you into the country or not and stamp your passport.

It has become a bit of a protracted procedure over the last few years as security in the USA has tightened up significantly, but just smile and be normal and maybe make some chit chat with the security person and you will be fine. They will be taking your fingerprints electronically and taking your picture with a camera that looks like a web cam, but no big deal, it's all for our protection.

The second flight then becomes an internal flight, so when you arrive in Las Vegas you can whizz through to collect your luggage with no waiting around in queues for customs. You will have to wait for the luggage to be unloaded of course, but you can almost relax now – you're nearly there. There may be a 10-15 minute wait for your luggage, so use this time to nip outside and check out the shuttle buses or taxis.

Coping with jet lag

If you're visiting Las Vegas from the UK or Europe, make sure you get plenty of sleep the night before as the city is eight hours behind. It is going to be a long day, but it will be worth it! Also, we suggest you try and stay awake until at least nine or ten o'clock in the evening after arriving, as this will help with the jet-lag. We tend to go for a walk around the casino, as it stops us falling asleep in the room too early.

We have found that on the outward trip to Vegas the jet lag works to our advantage. We find ourselves wide awake early in the morning for a few days until we adapt to the local time zone. But this can be a good thing, as there is lots to see and you will be keen to check out the hotel and the strip, so being up and awake with the larks and the dawn chorus for a few days is ideal.

For us, the jet lag on the return trip has always been worse, so be prepared for it. You won't feel like doing much for a couple of days after you arrive home, so if possible don't plan on going back to work the following day. We tend to feel like zombies for a few days after our return.

Travel insurance

Travel Insurance for medical emergencies is always advisable, especially when travelling to America. There is no national free health system, so falling ill can become expensive. Even a visit to a dentist to deal with a toothache will cost a few hundred dollars.

Travel insurance is easy to find on price comparison websites or your local insurance broker. Print off a copy of the policy and the phone number and have it with you at all times.

Travel money

While travellers' cheques are still accepted in most places worldwide, they are rapidly becoming a thing of the past. If you like to use them they can easily be cashed with any cashier in the casinos.

It's nice to have some money in your pocket upon arrival, so we always take around $200 with us. This is useful for the shuttle bus or taxi from the airport, and other things after arriving at the hotel.

Our debit cards work well here and allow us to draw money from the ATMs when ever we need it. My general rule is to buy goods with a credit card (as they will be insured) and draw cash with a debit card. Drawing cash on a credit card will work out very expensive!

We prefer to draw cash from ATMs at banks such as Wells Fargo or Bank of America, but there are many ATMs around the casinos and in the shops too.

They all make a charge for the convenience, which is around $5. For this reason you may want to draw enough cash to last for several days, as drawing small amounts of cash every couple of days will incur a charge every time. I certainly don't mind paying a couple of $5 charges throughout the duration of our stay, it's far better than carrying hundreds of dollars around.

WHERE TO STAY

Hotels and resort fees

The next job on the list is to book your accommodation. How many nights you book and where depends on how you want to plan your trip. Some questions you need to ask yourself are - will you be staying in Las Vegas for the duration of your trip? Will you be staying in the same hotel or moving to a different hotel half way through the holiday - or maybe even using several hotels?

Whichever way you want to do it, you should always book the first few nights before going. We always book the first two or three nights, so we can relax in the sun and chill out when we arrive before we start exploring away from the Strip.

We always explore beyond the Vegas Valley itself, as you will see from the pages that follow, but you may be content to stay within Las Vegas on your first trip, as there is plenty to see and do to keep you occupied for the duration. We didn't start venturing out of the valley until at least our second trip, but then it was still only short distances such as Death Valley and the Hoover Dam. These can be explored in a day easily in a car or truck.

The Grand Canyon can also be done in a day, and it's a fantastic drive through some open country taking in a lovely little town called Williams which stands on the historic Route 66. But this will be a long day, so be prepared. And you will have to enjoy driving to do it. More about that later.

Back to booking the hotel. One thing you need be aware of are **resort fees**. Many hotels in Las Vegas apply these fees on a nightly basis. They are charged to your credit card when you check out.

For a short time a few years ago these fees were known as energy surcharges, but whatever they are called it amounts to the same thing.

They cover use of the facilities, such as the pool and spa, a gym if the hotel has one and sometimes the internet. To me this is just a marketing ploy - it is all done to make the initial nightly fee look cheaper, shame on them!

Not all the hotels charge resort fees, so you need to check if the hotel you want to book is going to spring some surprise charges on you upon checkout.

So you book your hotel online and the price for the room is charged to your credit or debit card (I would always suggest using a credit card, because if anything goes wrong you should be covered by insurance, this goes for the flight and car rental too). Then after spending a few nights at the hotel, you check out and are suddenly presented with the resort fee bill, which can amount to quite a sum if you have stayed in the hotel for several days.

Resort fees can range from $4-$25 per night, depending on the hotel. The hotel's own websites should inform you how much the nightly fees are, but if not there is a good website which will tell you exactly what resort fee each hotel charges at **i4vegas.com**. This website is very easy to use and often delivers the best prices as well as good detailed descriptions, the location of the hotel and some pictures.

There are many hotels which do not charge any resort fee, but still have the same facilities. The choice is yours. It's just nice to know exactly what to expect when checking out of the hotel.

I have to say that we have only ever seen these resort fees charged in Las Vegas and around the Vegas valley. We have never seen such fees outside Las Vegas.

The hotels in Las Vegas and the valley are cheaper on a week night than at the weekend. For this reason we tend to arrive on a Tuesday if possible, or Wednesday at the latest, so we can chill out for a couple of days and then check out and go exploring on the Friday. Hotel prices rocket on Friday and Saturday night. So, Friday is when we will pick up our rental car. Starting to make sense now, isn't it?

Very few hotel rooms in Vegas have coffee-making facilities or fridges. For this reason we always take a small travel kettle so we can brew up in the room whenever we want. Walking down to the coffee shop every time you want a cuppa, especially first thing in the morning, can be exasperating, and using room service continually becomes very expensive. Throw some tea bags and a small supply of coffee in your suitcase when leaving home, to last until you can find a supermarket.

EXPLORING LAS VEGAS

Most of the main themed hotels are on the Strip and Downtown, the main parts of Vegas, where you will find most of the tourists most of the time. The strip is around four miles in length, and at the north end is Downtown Las Vegas.

Downtown is the old part of Vegas, consisting of Freemont Street, where you can see the Freemont Street experience in the evening, with a fantastic light show and lots going on every night. There are some more nice hotels situated Downtown so these are always an option. But remember, the Downtown hotels are quite a trek from the airport compared to the others at the south end of the Strip, and some don't have a pool.

The Strip is basically a dual carriageway with about five lanes each side. Most of the hotels lie along it. There are many walkways and pedestrian crossings to get you from one side to the other. This is not at all like a British motorway, with traffic hurtling up and down at great speed. The traffic is much slower and more chilled, and they actually respect pedestrians and will give way to you.

By the way, in case you were wondering why it's called the Strip, it used to be the runway for the airport many years ago when the downtown region was the main part of Las Vegas. Around 1948 they opened McCarran International Airport, as they realised they were going to need something bigger to cope with the influx of visitors as Las Vegas was becoming ever popular.

The hotels along the Strip are truly extraordinary. Nineteen of the world's 25 biggest hotels (by number of rooms) are on the Strip, with the staggering total of over 67,000 rooms between them.

I mentioned that the hotels tend to be themed. In fact they are almost all themed, especially the ones located on or near to the Strip. The famous Caesar's Palace of course has a Roman theme, and New York New York has a New York theme, the outside appearing like New York skyscrapers. You will discover many others, each unique in its own way.

It's quite a challenge to describe what these hotels are like inside, but I will do my best. There is so much on offer that you could spend your whole holiday inside any one of them and never leave. There is everything you could possibly need inside them, from different types of restaurants to hair salons and shops where you can buy newspapers and milk. There is entertainment by the bucketload, and of course each hotel has a huge casino, which is where they want you to lose your money. But remember that just because you stay in a particular hotel there is no pressure to gamble or even go into the casino if you don't want to. You can walk through and just watch what's going on, if that's all you wish to do.

When people ask, I usually try to convey the vastness of these hotels by saying that each of them is the size of a huge shopping centre. They cover several acres and most have several hundred rooms and suites, if not thousands.

If you do have a flutter in the casino, whether on the slot machines or at the card tables, remember you can drink for free while you are gambling. Yes, for free! So if you'd like a little tipple, just call over the cocktail waitress and tell her what you want from the bar and she will bring it to you. You may want to give her a dollar for her trouble, as this is why she is there serving you in the first place, and of course if you don't drink alcohol she will always bring you a coffee or a soft drink - maybe even some breakfast if you ask nicely. The only thing you definitely don't want her to bring you is bad luck, if you're gambling.

You won't find any clocks in the casinos. All the casinos are open 24 hours and nothing looks any different at 3 am from the way it did at 5 pm, except that there are maybe not so many people. Generally, if you stood in the middle of a casino and had no idea what time of day it was, it would be difficult to guess it from the surroundings.

We have been visiting Las Vegas for the past fifteen years, and we've lost count of exactly how many times we have landed at McCarran airport. I can't quite put my finger on what attracts us to this place. It is definitely not the gambling, as we only dabble a little now and again in the hope of winning the big one. Without the gambling this place would probably not exist, as this is what brings in the tourists and the tax dollars for the state of Nevada.

The sunny weather is definitely a big attraction, but we also love the openness of the area and the surrounding desert. Even when we are on the Strip, this place still does not feel like a big city. In fact no part of the Vegas valley feels like a big city, which is one of the things we love as we are not keen on busy cities. Concrete jungles make us feel claustrophobic. But hop into a car here and within five minutes you can almost be in the middle of nowhere.

The weather in Las Vegas is wonderful. It is warm here for nine months of the year, and gets extremely hot during the months of July and August. It can be so hot then that you could fry an egg and even a rasher or two of bacon on the bonnet (sorry, hood) of the car. Maybe I'll try beans and mushrooms next time and report back in the next book.

The average daily high temperature in July and August is around 105°, but we have seen it even hotter. The Vegas valley sometimes experiences freak high temperatures too. I remember vividly back in May of 2003 coming to Las Vegas after going to the Indy 500 at Indianapolis. A friend and I were on the Strip at midnight, and according to the thermometer outside Caesar's Palace it was 108° even then.

September is our favourite month, when temperatures average around 95°, which is just about right for us. When we come in September our suitcases are almost empty, as it is an ideal time to hit the shops with all the summer gear being on sale.

Anyway, I have digressed already and we have only just started. Now to the scenery around Vegas.

The Strip

As I said earlier, this book is designed to help you escape the main tourist bubble and see some of the sights in and around the Vegas valley. But no book about Las Vegas would be complete without a little about the Strip and what can be found there.

The Las Vegas strip lies almost smack bang in the middle of the valley and is approximately four miles in length. It stretches from the Stratosphere Tower at the north end to Mandalay Bay in the south.

The strip and Downtown are the main parts of Las Vegas, where most of the large themed hotels and casinos are located. In fact Downtown, the old part of Las Vegas, is in the city of Las Vegas, while the Strip is actually located in the township of Paradise. Collectively though, it is all known as Las Vegas.

The Strip is so called because this is where Las Vegas airport was originally located. It remained in operation until 1948, when it served Downtown, until it became so busy that they moved it to its current location at the south end of the Strip. The airport is now named after a former US senator of Nevada, Patrick McCarran. The airport handles eleven hundred flights daily and as soon as you step out of the aircraft and into the terminal you will be confronted with noisy slot machines.

Whichever hotel you choose to stay in, you will almost certainly be doing a lot of walking if you want to see all the Strip has to offer, so I suggest a good pair of walking shoes or trainers would be appropriate, or you are going to end up with sore feet and maybe even blisters.

The first time we came to Vegas we were so excited on the first day that we got carried away looking at all the lights and attractions and didn't realise how far we were walking. We both plodded from the Luxor, where we were staying, down as far as Caesar's Palace and back again, and went in and out of almost every hotel along the way. If my memory serves me correctly it was around seven hours of walking. Needless to say we both ended up with big blisters on our feet, which bugged us for the next two weeks of our stay! At least it's a good way to stay fit if you have the right footwear.

If you get tired of walking, look out for a double-decker bus called the Deuce Bus. It will have Deuce on the front and rear of the bus and runs 24 hours a day, seven days a week, stopping at all the hotels along the Strip and Downtown. There are lots of these buses running at any one time, so you won't have to wait long. Make sure you have the correct money for the machine, as the driver does not give change. It's a flat fare of $3, no matter how far your journey, and the machine in the bus only accepts dollar bills.

The Strip is a very large and busy road and in some places it is five or six lanes wide. At first glance you would be forgiven for thinking it is dangerous, which it is if you step out in front of a car or bus, but there are plenty of footbridges and pedestrian crossings where you can cross the road safely and the traffic is relatively slow as there are traffic lights in abundance.

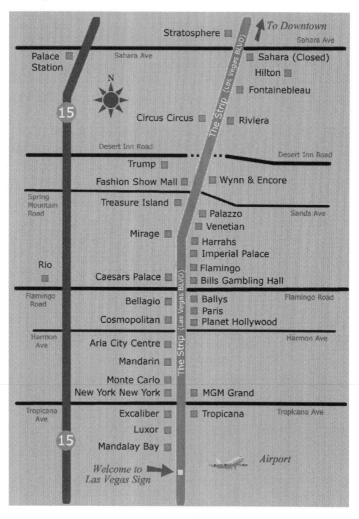

Map of The Strip

Hotel highlights

I am not going to talk about every hotel as there are just too many to mention, but I will cover some of the highlights and hopefully give people some idea of what to expect and some of the things to look out for when they visit Vegas.

Starting at the north end of the Strip is the **Stratosphere**. You can't miss this one – it's the one with the tower reaching almost 1200 feet into the sky.

If you have a head for heights there is a great view of the whole of Las Vegas and the Vegas valley from the top, especially impressive at night when all the lights are ablaze. You will also find several thrill rides at the top, but be warned - they are not for the faint-hearted, as some of them will suspend you over the side of the tower. My favourite is the Big Shot, although Nuala won't come on it with me. When it shoots you up into the air the tower below disappears from view and for a few seconds you feel you are suspended over 1200 feet above the Strip, with nothing between you and the ground.

Across the road is the **Sahara**, now closed and looking a bit sorry for itself though it was a popular hotel for many years. This corner of Las Vegas Boulevard will look strange after they bring down this iconic hotel with dynamite.

Heading south you will find **Circus Circus**, which in my opinion is a bit dated now with its circus theme and main entrance shaped like a big top. The hotel boasts an impressive indoor theme park called Adventuredome with 25 thrilling rides and attractions which include a full-size roller coaster.

Further south we find the **Fashion Show Mall**, great for shopping with a huge number of shops and a well-stocked food court for something to eat. If this place was a hotel, I think Nuala and I would stay here, especially during the sales!

Immediately opposite the Fashion Show Mall is the **Wynn Hotel**, which boasts its very own golf course in the back yard, for guests only. If you like to play golf then don't worry about that as there are several other courses around the valley.

Cross over Spring Mountain Road from the Fashion Show Mall and you're at **Treasure Island**, or **TI** as it is now known. The theme here used to be pirates, and the galleons out front would put on a great show with a battle between the British and the Americans, with a dramatic sinking of one of the ships as the finale. Now, along with the name change, this seems to have changed too. The ships still do battle, but the theme seems to be centred more on scantily-clad girls. I preferred the original show, but it is still enjoyable and can be watched from the side of the road for free!

Next up on the same side of the road is **The Mirage**, with an active 'volcano' that erupts every few minutes in the evening. Inside you will find a huge aquarium in the lobby and a dolphin habitat to the rear. We found this to be a bit expensive, especially for a family with two or more children. They used to have white tigers behind glass inside the hotel, but they are long gone after an accident on stage when one of the performers was injured by one of the animals.

Immediately across the Strip from The Mirage you will see **the Venetian**. Now this place just has to be seen, in all its glory and extravagance. There is no way I can do it justice with words alone, so I am not going to bother trying. In fact I can't do any of these hotels justice by talking about them, they all have to be seen and experienced to be appreciated.

Inside the Venetian Hotel

When stepping inside the front door of the Venetian you start to get a taster for what is to come, with mirror-finished marble floors beneath your feet and impressive Da Vinci murals on the ceilings. Inside you can take a romantic ride on the Grand Canal in a gondola with your very own singing gondolier, or if that's not your thing then pop along to St Mark's Square, which is next to the canal. Here there are many shops and restaurants and even some free entertainment to keep you amused. It is very easy to get lost inside the vastness of some of these hotels, but then that's all part of the fun!

A little further south is the **Flamingo**. You should recognise this one from the pink flamingo-shaped flashing lights out front. The wildlife habitat inside is very impressive. It is set among waterfalls and streams and there are many kinds of birds and fish as well as, of course, flamingos.

On the opposite side of the Strip is the famous **Caesar's Palace**. With its Roman theme, this place never fails to impress. The pool area is called the Garden of the Gods and has eight different pools, where you will find yourself surrounded by large columns, impressive statues and an 18-foot waterfall. The Colosseum hosts many big stars, so check out who's playing.

Dancing fountains at the Bellagio Hotel

Next to Caesar's you will find The **Bellagio**. This place is probably best known for the dancing fountains in front of the hotel. They can be seen from the Strip for free without entering the hotel, and are one of the highlights of Las Vegas. They dance to different classical and

Broadway tunes and put on their show every fifteen minutes. Nuala will stand and watch them all evening, but once or twice is enough for me!

Cross the Strip again to the **Paris Hotel**. You can't miss this one, because it has a half-scale exact replica of the Eiffel Tower which rises above the Las Vegas skyline. You can take an elevator ride to the top for another great view of the whole of the Vegas valley.

Moving south again, we come to a large crossroads where Tropicana Avenue crosses over the Strip. This is a huge area of activity, with four equally interesting hotels, one on each corner. The **Tropicana** is the oldest of the four and is looking a bit dated these days, but it does have a good comedy club if you feel like a good laugh one evening. Another good comedy club, 'Improv', can be found at Harrah's Hotel.

The **MGM Grand** is the largest hotel in Las Vegas and the third largest in the world, with a staggering 6852 rooms. Its attractive greenish glow is a noted feature of the Vegas skyline at night. Inside on the casino floor you will find a large lion habitat, which is free to visit. The lion connection comes of course from the big screen, where Leo has been roaring at the beginning of MGM's movies for the best part of a century.

Lions at the MGM Grand

The lions don't live at the habitat – their home is on a ranch several miles away, and different lions are brought in every day. Perhaps they are whisked in by chauffeur-driven limo while sipping champers! They are certainly treated exceptionally well. The lions turn up around mid morning (when you're such a famous quadruped there's no need to get up early). The keepers enter the enclosure with the lions to play with them, and this can all be watched through thick glass. Getting up close to the glass makes for some great photos. You may have to drag yourself away, as watching these lions can become very addictive.

New York New York

The next hotel on the crossroads here is **New York New York**, so good they named it twice. The front of this hotel has to be my favourite for kerb appeal because it looks just like the New York skyline, complete with the Statue of Liberty parked right out front. Inside, to the rear of the casino, you will find narrow little streets with trees and buildings and even steam coming up from the manhole covers in the street. It's a great setting to sit and enjoy some English fish and chips from the little shop on the corner. If you are as fond of roller-coasters as I am, the one here at New York New York should tick all the right boxes. It is very fast and the drops are big. It also mimics a jet fighter's barrel roll, so strap in and have fun. Just inside the front door can be found the **Coyote Ugly** bar from the movie with the same name, complete with people dancing on the bar. It seems to be very busy all the time.

The Excalibur Hotel

The fourth hotel here on the crossroads is the **Excalibur**. With the theme of King Arthur and Camelot, it looks like a mystical castle from the outside with its red and blue turrets. This place has plenty to offer. I still can't figure out why they called it Excalibur after King Arthur's sword and not Camelot after where he lived, but they must have had their reasons!

Now we come to the **Luxor**, or the Pyramid hotel as some people may know it. It opened in 1993 and is the second largest hotel in Vegas. The pyramid structure is very distinctive and it is equally impressive inside. The rooms are built into the skin of the pyramid, giving it a hollow effect when you walk inside.

We stayed here once several years ago and I am glad we did, just to experience this place first hand. In each corner of the pyramid is an inclinator which goes up to the rooms - so called as they don't go straight up like a conventional elevator but rise at an angle. The light on top of the pyramid, which is powered up at night is equivalent to 240,000 light bulbs, and they tell us to save energy!

At the very south of the Strip is the **Mandalay Bay Hotel**. In our opinion, this place has by far the best pool complex in Las Vegas. It covers eleven acres and there is a wave pool, a lazy river and even a huge beach. You won't find the sea anywhere nearby of course, but maybe the next hotel they build here in Vegas will rectify that one and have an ocean. In Vegas, you never know what they will try to do next. There is even a poolside casino here, in case you feel like a quick hand of blackjack while sunbathing. As with all the hotels you need to be a guest to access the pool areas, but you are free to explore the rest of the hotel, attractions and casino area.

Inside the Mandalay Bay you will find the **Shark Reef Aquarium**, another great experience if you enjoy sea life. There are all kinds of sharks as well as turtles, giant rays, piranha and even the rare golden crocodile. Qualified divers can grasp the opportunity to dive with the sharks too, although personally I would rather stay in the dry behind the glass.

We are now at the southern end of the Strip, but Las Vegas Boulevard continues on with one or two more hotels if you want to explore further. There are also many more hotels scattered around the valley, but you will ideally need a vehicle to visit them.

All the hotels in Vegas have free parking for guests and visitors, with the possible exception of one or two hotels in the Downtown area. Self-parking is clearly marked when entering the parking area. They all have valet parking too, which I like to use sometimes after having a hard day's driving in the leather throne, or if we have just been shopping and cleaned out one of the local shopping malls. It is customary to tip the valet a dollar or two for their trouble when collecting the car.

The famous **'Welcome to Las Vegas' sign** can be found just south of the Mandalay Bay Hotel in the centre of the road. There is a parking area for cars and coaches in the centre next to the sign, which can only be accessed when heading south, so get into the left lane when passing the Mandalay Bay ready to turn in. This is the sign that most people visit to take pictures, and we have seen many wedding couples having their pictures taken here.

There are two other 'Welcome to Las Vegas' signs. One can be found just north of the Stratosphere Tower and the other is on the Boulder Highway, which is around twenty minutes' drive east of the Strip.

I can only think of one thing that this place is missing, and that's a water park. There used to be a Wet n' Wild at the north end of the Strip next to the Sahara Hotel, but it disappeared about ten years ago. This may be because all the hotels have their own impressive water havens, which seem to become more lavish with every new hotel built, so perhaps they feel a water park is superfluous.

Downtown Las Vegas - the Freemont Street experience

Downtown can be found just north of the Las Vegas Strip and is widely known as the Freemont Street experience. From the Strip you can grab a taxi or just hop on the Deuce Bus, which will drop you just where you need to go and collect you from the same place when you want to return. As previously mentioned, the Deuce Bus runs 24 hours a day up and down the Strip and to Downtown, and you will need the exact money - $3 in $1 dollar bills for the machine, the driver gives no change.

Downtown is the original Las Vegas and the business centre for Nevada. Many years ago, before the Strip became so popular with tourists due to development of the themed hotels and other attractions, this is where people would come to gamble and have a good time.

Downtown Las Vegas – the Fremont Street experience

I would advise a trip to Downtown at night, as there is a fantastic video and audio show every hour, on the hour, which starts at sundown and goes on until midnight. It uses the world's largest video screen, suspended 90 feet in the air and covering four blocks – that's 1500 feet in length. The huge video canopy runs the whole length of Freemont Street, so you will have a good view wherever you stand.

Downtown Las Vegas – the video canopy

The shows on the canopy are computer generated and last for six minutes and when the show starts, the casinos switch off all their neon lights to allow the canopy to come alive. There are side shows, plenty of shops and live entertainment every night, all for free (the entertainment is free, not the merchandise of course).

Downtown is also known as the "Glitter Gulch", because there are said to be over 12 million lights. Freemont Street has been closed to traffic since 1995.

There is also a cluster of casinos here, all within a short walk of each other. Check out the pool area in the **Golden Nugget** - I know I said earlier that you won't have access to a hotel's pool area unless you are a guest, but if you're here in the evening you will be able to wander in and see the fish tank in the centre. It is called **The Tank** (not very original but to the point I guess) and there is a water slide (guests only) which takes them through the middle of the Tank on the way down.

Around the corner in the lobby you will find the world's largest gold nugget on display. Known as the **Hand of Faith**, the nugget was found in Australia and put on display here in 1981.

A few paces down one of the side streets is an outside movie theatre.

We noticed on several occasions that they only seemed to be showing black and white movies so we didn't participate, it all looked slightly pointless anyway as we could see the movie from outside the railings.

That reminds me, I have only ever found one drive-in movie in all my time in America, and it can be found a short drive from the Strip. It is located on "West Carey Avenue" just off "North Rancho drive" and right next to the Fiesta Rancho hotel. There are several screens and it is open nightly.

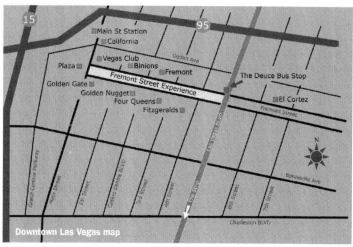

The Las Vegas Monorail

The Las Vegas Monorail, on the east side of the Strip, first opened in 2004. The 3.9 mile route connects the MGM Grand to the south with the Sahara in the north. Although the Sahara is now closed the station is still open and can be accessed on Paradise Road, a short walk from the Strip.

The Monorail consists of seven stations, each station serving several hotels and locations on the Strip. Because the stations are located to the rear of the hotels and the hotels themselves are so vast, it can be quite a long walk from the Strip to the Monorail.

There isn't a great deal to see when riding the Monorail apart from the back views of the hotels and some large concrete car parks, so don't expect a scenic journey. Though people who like golf may get a glimpse of the golf course at the Wynn Hotel.

The trains run every 5 or 10 minutes, so there's never long to wait. They also run until 2 am on weekdays and 3 am at weekends. The carriages are clean and have air-conditioning, and there are always security guards at every station, although we have never seen one on the train itself.

On the west side of the Strip there are three smaller trams which connect different hotels. While these are free to use, the monorail is NOT free. It will cost several dollars each for a one-way trip regardless of the length of your journey. A day pass can be bought for unlimited use but this is only economically viable if you intend to make several journeys.

Tickets can be booked online cheaper, but this is only useful if you have planned to use the monorail ahead of time and have access to the internet.

The monorail also stops at the **Hilton Hotel** and the **Las Vegas Convention Centre**, which are located away from the Strip on Paradise Road. So if you are in town for a convention and staying on the Strip this is very convenient.

Shopping in Las Vegas

If you are like us, you will be looking forward to some American retail therapy, and Las Vegas is a good place to satisfy that craving. I mentioned the **Fashion Show Mall** earlier when I was talking about the Strip, and this is a good place to start, especially if you don't want to venture too far from the Strip. It is known as the Fashion Show Mall because inside on the lower level you will find a catwalk and lighting that is used for fashion shows. There are several large department stores here and over 250 shops and restaurants, as well as a large food court located at the front on the upper level.

The Fashion Show Mall is centrally located on the Strip immediately opposite the Wynn Hotel. There is a huge grey disk at the front called The Cloud - I have no idea why, as it looks more like a UFO to me. The

Fashion Show is in fairly easy walking distance of most of the hotels on the Strip.

Remember that if you are planning to walk back to the hotel after your shopping spree you may have lots of heavy bags filled with goodies, so you may want to hail a cab or jump on the Deuce Bus instead.

Many of the Strip hotels also have their own small shopping areas, such as the **Miracle Mile** shops in **Planet Hollywood** and the **Forum shops** at **Caesar's Palace**, to mention just two. By 'small' I mean smaller than the Malls (just) though there is nothing small about them. They are a completely different experience from the malls, offering their own selection of shops and themes. But be aware that the price tags are likely to be higher here than in a local mall or outlet.

Another thing to mention is that if you buy things like cigarettes, milk, suntan cream or pretty much anything else from the convenience shops in the hotels, you are going to pay top dollar. If you can get to a supermarket or a pharmacy you will save a fortune. Several pharmacies can be found on the Strip, and they are a much cheaper option than the hotel shops. You won't be able to buy cigarettes at the supermarkets - you will need to buy these from a smoke shop to get the best price, or if you are desperate go to a gas station. Some pharmacies sell cigarettes. The cheapest place to buy them is on the aircraft, so if you're a smoker think ahead and stock up.

Another popular place with tourists is **Las Vegas Premium Outlets South**, which you will find about two miles south of Mandalay Bay on South Las Vegas Boulevard, just past Warm Springs Road. There is also a **Las Vegas Premium Outlets North**, two miles north of the Stratosphere Tower. Just follow Las Vegas Boulevard north and turn left on to Charleston, then turn right just before the I-15 into Grand Central Parkway. Both of these are easy to find by car, but my preference would be the south one, as it is a much more straightforward drive. If you don't have a car then any taxi driver will know exactly where to go. You can also check to see if the hotel where you are staying lays on any transport for shopping excursions, as many of them do.

You will find taxis lined up outside all the shopping malls, so getting back to the hotel again is never going to be a problem. Here you won't find any department stores, but there are around 150 shops, many with well-known brand names.

Town Square is a popular place to shop, and it's a very short distance from the Strip. Just past Mandalay Bay heading south you will see it on your right. It's very easy to park and covers 117 acres. This place is meant to resemble a European town and the buildings are all different, with ideas taken from all over Europe. There is a park area in the centre with little walkways and bridges, and there always seems to be something happening here on the grass in the summer months. There are also several restaurants with the option of eating al fresco. The shops are all relatively close together, so no excessive walking is required. There is even an 18-screen movie theatre.

If you like ice cream then don't miss **Yogurtland** - we came here more than once just for the frozen yogurt. I wasn't too sure at first, but Nuala told me it's just like ice cream, and now I'm hooked.

If you want to try a shopping experience that is a little more laid back, where you are more likely to be surrounded by locals than tourists, there are three options. The first is the **Boulevard Mall**. You will find this one on Maryland Parkway, which runs parallel to the Strip on the east side. From the Strip head east on Flamingo, then after about one mile turn left on to Maryland Parkway. You will find the Mall on your right just after Katie Avenue. There are approximately 170 shops and department stores, such as Macy's, JC Penny, Dillards and Sears to keep you amused. We have been here many times and my wallet always takes a bashing.

The second place is the **Meadows Mall**, with 150 shops, including the same big names. This place offers a similar experience to the Boulevard Mall. Getting here again depends where you are staying, but from the Strip I would start off by heading west on Flamingo, go over the I-15 and then just past the Rio hotel turn right on to Valleyview Boulevard. Keep going straight on this road and after about five miles you will see the Meadows Mall on your left.

The third place, and our favourite place to shop in Vegas, is the **Galleria Mall**, or **Galleria at Sunset**, as some people call it. This place is a bit further away from the Strip but well worth the extra miles. You will find several department stores and around 150 shops spread over two levels to keep you occupied. There's also a large food court with lots of choice, although when we come here it is the Philly cheese steak every time for us. There is always plenty of parking, as there is at all the malls, and security services patrol the car parks at all times, as they do in the hotel car parks too.

There is more than one way to get to the Galleria Mall from the Strip, but I am going to tell you the one I think is easiest. It will take around 20 minutes. Head south past Mandalay Bay and take a left on to Sunset Road, the first road past the airport. This will take you along the south side of the airport. Before you get to where the runway to your left ends, you will see an area where you can pull in and watch the planes landing. If you are new to driving in the USA, **here's a small tip**. The lane in the centre between the yellow lines is a turning lane which allows you to pull in to make a left turn. Be sure not to pull in front of someone else making a turn coming from the other direction.

Continue along Sunset for a fair distance until you come to a junction where Sunset road turns to the right. You will see Mountain Vista going to the left. Continue to follow Sunset for another two miles and the Galleria Mall will appear to your left, almost immediately opposite Sunset Station Casino and Hotel.

There is one more place to mention, and that is **Fashion Outlets of Las Vegas**. This small mall is about a 45-minute drive south of Vegas down the I-15 in a place called Primm. I will be talking about Primm and explaining how to get there later on. You won't find any department stores here but there are some top names and over 100 shops in total. I would describe the shopping experience here as very relaxing, with all the shops arranged in a circular shape, making it very easy to navigate.

Getting married in Las Vegas
Licence fee $55

Thousands of people every year decide to tie the knot in the glamorous setting of Las Vegas. There are countless wedding chapels dotted around the valley, plus several at both ends of the Strip. Many of the hotels have their own wedding chapels too. They provide all kinds of themes, including getting married in your birthday suit, sitting on a Harley Davidson motorcycle or even being married by 'Elvis'!

If you plan on getting married here then you may want to avoid popular holiday periods, such as St Valentine's Day or New Year. Don't be surprised if you are herded in and out like sheep on these days. Only a small amount of time will be allotted to each wedding, as they do so many each day. They will supply the witnesses though, so it's not all bad!

Before getting married, both the bride and groom will need to appear in person to get a marriage licence from the **Clark County Marriage Licence Bureau**, at the County Courthouse, South 3rd Street. This can be found in the Downtown area north of the Stratosphere Tower.

The Las Vegas Valley

Las Vegas is situated in the middle of the Mojave desert in a huge valley approximately 600 square miles in extent, almost completely surrounded by mountains. To the west are the Spring Mountains, where Mount Charleston can be found, while the Sheep and Las Vegas mountains lie to the north, the Frenchman mountains to the east and the McCullough mountains to the south.

The first European to set foot in the Vegas valley was a man named Rafael Rivera, back in 1829. He stumbled across a valley covered in wild grass and lush meadows, the result of a plentiful water supply. This is where the name Las Vegas comes from - it is Spanish for 'The Meadows'.

I often wonder what it must have been like for this guy travelling across America all those years ago. I have been known to complain on the odd occasion about the length of the journey to Las Vegas and the unbearable summer heat when I arrive, but Rivera and the people he was travelling with must have been travelling for weeks by boat and then by mule, with no air-conditioned hotel to cool off in when he arrived.

Las Vegas is very tourist friendly and the locals who serve visitors couldn't be more helpful. You may say well of course they would be, because they want our cash, but in my experience travelling around America I don't believe this to be the case. When they say 'Have a nice day!', in most cases they really mean it.

In no way does this place deserve the title of Sin City. You will have to look very hard to find anything sordid about it. Of course there are some seedy areas, just like any city, and I could tell you where to find them, but that's not what this book is about. For the most part you won't have to worry about it. You see the occasional billboard on the side of a truck, and certain people on a very short section of the Strip give out cards with girls' phone numbers, but that's the most you will have to worry about. Just ignore them and don't let them spoil your day.

You could describe Las Vegas as an adult Disneyland, or an adult playground. There are bars and restaurants everywhere, including lots of al fresco eating, roller coasters and other rides, swimming and chilling by the pool, shopping, nightclubs and of course lots of gambling, if that's your thing. You won't see too many children here, so if you're not a lover of noisy offspring, this place can be heaven.

Exploring beyond Las Vegas

We leave the valley on the Friday and head off on our sightseeing. We normally end up travelling around for a week or so, staying at motels along the way. One time we couldn't find a motel, so we rented a pre-pitched tent just outside Yosemite National Park. This is not usually necessary as there are motels everywhere. Just be sure to ask the price, and don't be afraid to haggle a little with the person behind the counter when you arrive. This person may well be the owner, especially if it is a smaller motel, and most of the time they are happy to knock a few dollars off the price if you ask nicely, especially if it's getting late in the evening and there's less chance of renting the room to someone else. The bigger motels are a bit more tricky to negotiate with, but have a go anyway - it sometimes works.

One thing I must mention is that we always take a laptop with us. It fits nicely in the rucksack for the journey, as most rucksacks now have a laptop compartment, and it proves invaluable. Most of the motels we have stayed at have free WiFi, and the laptop is very handy for planning a route for the next day and also for booking the hotel back in Las Vegas after our trip.

The hotels in the Vegas Valley are now catching up with the times and most have WiFi, but you need to do your homework as only a few of them give it free. One or two even use a third party to supply their guests with the internet, which we don't like and would never use as it involves giving our credit card details and it can be expensive. The fewer people you have to give your credit card details to the better.

We also use the laptop to download the day's photos from our cameras, which is very handy. It's good fun to relax in the motel in the evening with a coffee and something to eat after a hard day's sightseeing, flicking through to see which pictures look good and which need deleting.

ON THE ROAD

Motoring in the USA

If you like road trips and relish the open road, there are plenty of day trips from Las Vegas that will satisfy your craving. Almost everywhere we go when leaving Vegas leads us to the open road and scenery as far as the eye can see. So it's a good idea to rent a car during your stay.

Notice I said rent - not hire. In America hiring a car means a car and driver, so make sure you talk about renting.

If you don't wish to rent a car there are still many places which are accessible using public transport or by local tour operators.

Driving on the right will be fairly straightforward if you're used to driving in continental Europe, but Brits will need to get used to it first time around. It's surprisingly easy after a short time, as long as you don't relax too much and forget where you are, particularly when you're driving off after a stop and there's no other traffic around to remind you. The roads tend to be bigger in the USA than in Europe and some of the junctions and intersections are huge, and can be quite daunting if you are not used to them, so pay attention.

I don't want to put anyone off driving in the USA, because once you get used to the size of the roads and driving on the right it quickly becomes a pleasure. I have noticed during my time driving here that there seems to be far more respect for other drivers and pedestrians than I have ever experienced in England. I love driving in the States, as the roads are relatively clear of traffic compared to our congested nightmare at home. In Las Vegas, a traffic jam is more than four cars waiting at a set of lights. There is plenty of traffic around Vegas, but it seems to flow easily.

When you leave the city and the more built-up areas, the roads are much the same size as at home in England. The people seem to have more patience and very few people speed here, so I find driving is much more relaxing than at home and I can drive all day without getting stressed out once.

Talking about speeding, I should mention that if you get caught speeding you will get a fine, but if you are caught within a section of roadworks the fine will be doubled, so be warned! The local police and highway patrol seem to pitch camp at the roadworks with their speed guns.

There are a couple of things I should point out which you should find very useful. The first is that you can turn right at a red light, as long as there's nothing approaching from your left. But keep an eye open for pedestrians, as they may have right of way if you are turning on a red. Keep an eye on the gantry above as well, as sometimes there will be a sign saying 'No Turn On Red', but not very often.

One type of junction which may confuse someone who has never driven in America before is the crossroads with no signals. This is a first come, first go scenario. I was very confused the first time I came across one of these, but I soon got the hang of it, and so will you. If you arrive at the give way line first the other driver will give way to you, but make sure you do the same.

Another thing that's worth mentioning is that when driving on a dual carriageway or interstate the law allows overtaking in all lanes. Most people adhere to the unwritten rule and pull over to the right, but if someone is going extra slow in the outside lane it's perfectly fine to 'undertake' on the inside.

In Europe and especially in the UK, there seems to have been an explosion in the roundabout population. They pop up everywhere imaginable, in places where no sane person would expect to find one. Fortunately, it's quite different in the USA. For the most part, your day in the big leather chair will be roundabout-free. But, someone from the roundabout creation committee in the UK must have relocated to the USA, as we have recently found two roundabouts in North Las Vegas and several in small towns in northern Arizona.

When you fill your vehicle with gas the way you're used to doing at home, you could be standing at the pump wondering why it is not working. This is because the pump will be dead until you go inside and pay. Yes, it's pay first, fuel second in the USA - driving off without paying is impossible. If you pay for thirty dollars of gas the pump will deliver exactly that.

Car rental

Renting a vehicle in Las Vegas is very easy. The rental companies have representatives at many hotels on the Strip and around the valley, along with a huge car rental complex at the airport.

As mentioned earlier, we never collect our vehicle from the airport as we prefer to have a few days to relax. We then collect it from the hotel we are staying at or one nearby. It would make no sense for us to collect a car from the airport on arrival only to leave it sitting in the car park for a couple of days while we chill out. Of course, if unlike us you plan to explore the valley as soon as you arrive or don't care about the added cost of it sitting there not being used, then by all means collect it from the airport upon arrival.

The rental car can be collected from a hotel and returned to the airport when leaving Vegas at no extra cost, or vice versa. If you return a vehicle to a different town or city then the rental companies treat this as a one-way rental and charge extra. This can be a considerable amount depending how far away you want to return the vehicle.

The process of renting a vehicle is very easy, but the insurance may be a little more complicated. Most car rental and third-party websites now include all the insurance necessary when renting a vehicle. Please make sure at the time of booking to have a glance through the terms and conditions to confirm this.

What you also need to be aware of is the **excess** they charge on these insurances when something goes wrong. It can be anything up to $2000 charged straight to your credit card. What you need to check for in the terms and conditions is **ZERO EXCESS**.

One other thing that's common and you need to be aware of is that these insurances sometimes do not cover certain parts of the vehicle, such as the window glass, damage to the wheels and tyres and the underside of the vehicle. So check the small print for this too.

We like to rent our vehicle before we leave home and mostly use two different websites. These are **Arguscarhire.com** and **Carhire3000.com** (now known as **Rentalcars.com**). Both these sites include the majority of the insurance required, including zero excess. They also, more often than not, deliver the best price too.

As always, make sure you read through the terms and conditions so you know exactly what's included. There are of course other sites to try, details of some of these can be found at the back of the book.

PLACES TO SEE

There are countless unforgettable sights to see within a day or so of Vegas if you don't mind a little driving – and as I said, it's a pleasure on these big, largely empty roads, once you get into the groove.

It's advisable to buy a good US road map when going on longer trips, or at least a good state map. Apart from its usefulness when you're out there, a map will be a great souvenir of your trip and helps in locating photos and planning your next visit.

State maps can be bought from gas stations and local shops. A good sense of direction is always helpful, along with some map-reading skills, because this country is so vast that if you go the wrong way it could cost you a great deal of time and fuel.

Here's my list of places to drive to, with details of any entrance fees and distances from Las Vegas.

Red Rock Canyon

Entrance fee $7 per vehicle

23 Miles

Red Rock Canyon is just over 20 miles to the west of Las Vegas – you can see it from the Strip if you know where to look. It's only about a 30-minute drive, but it makes for a striking contrast with the bright lights and bustle of the city. The 13-mile scenic loop around the canyon will give you views of beautiful sandstone rocks, which get their red colour from iron oxide. By driving the scenic loop you get to see many features of the canyon, but there are lots of hidden gems that can only be seen by taking the hiking trails that lead away from the road and into the mountains.

Red Rock Canyon

The rangers at the visitor centre will supply you with the information you need to find the best sights and trails to take. Some of the trails can take hours to complete, but there are shorter trails for people like us who don't want to be walking all day but still enjoy a good ramble across some rocks.

On certain trails you will be treated to cascading waterfalls and plentiful wildlife. You may be surprised how many different animals live out here in the desert, so keep your eyes open for roadrunners (yes they are not just cartoon creatures), ring-tail cats, ground squirrels, deer, sheep, burros (they look just like donkeys), kangaroo rats, kit foxes and rabbits. Kangaroo rats are quite small, but the huge bouncing rodent suggested by the name is enough to give any small child nightmares!

When we were here we saw many joggers and cyclists enjoying the quiet roads. Several people were rock climbing and in the distance you can see many hikers.

To reach Red Rock Canyon from the Strip there are two options. The first is to head south past Mandalay Bay and turn right on to the 215. Heading west, follow the 215 to exit 26 and turn left on to

Charleston Boulevard. A few miles up the road you will see the signs for Red Rock Canyon.

Depending on where you are staying, the second option is to head north on Las Vegas Boulevard past the Stratosphere Tower until you come to Charleston Boulevard, then turn left. This too is easy, but you may experience more traffic this way and definitely more traffic lights heading up Charleston Boulevard.

Bonnie Springs, Old Nevada
$20 per vehicle, up to 6 people
21 Miles

When you reach the end of the scenic loop in Red Rock Canyon you have two options. If you turn left, after a mile or two you will be back at the pay station where you entered the loop. My advice is to turn right back on to Charleston Boulevard and pay a visit to **Bonnie Springs**, an old western town nestling at the foot of the Spring Mountains. This road will eventually return you to the Las Vegas Boulevard a few miles south of Mandalay Bay.

Along this road you will find many hiking trails off to your right, but I'm guessing that we have had enough hiking by now. Bonnie Springs is off to your right a little way down the road. The old town has cowboy shows and you can even see a 'public hanging'. Despite this the people are very friendly and helpful and you are quite safe!

We have been here twice, and although this place looks a little worn around the edges - some would even call it cheesy - I would still say it's a good place to visit. The buildings appear somewhat run down, but then an old western town would appear that way. The motel could have done with some paint here and there the last time we visited, but the rooms inside were clean and tidy with everything you need if you plan to stay here. The ranch was built in 1843 and was used as a stopover for wagon trains heading to California. It became a tourist attraction in 1952.

You will find a restaurant, a cocktail lounge and even a zoo here. If you like horses they offer riding, and if you like stagecoaches you can ride in one of those too. It's an interesting place and makes a good combined trip with Red Rock canyon.

The Las Vegas Motor Speedway (LVMS)
16 Miles

The LVMS is only a 15-minute drive from the Las Vegas Strip, and if you are a motorsport fan as we are, there is no better place to be. It is a petrolhead's oasis in the desert. My guess is that the majority of visitors to Las Vegas don't realise the LVMS is so close to the Strip and miss out on all the high-octane action.

Las Vegas Motor Speedway

The main track is a 1.5 mile tri-oval with banking to the corners. From the stands you can get a complete view of all the action taking place without moving from your seat. The relatively new Neon Garage, which is behind the media centre in the infield, provides a great chance for fans to see their favourite teams and drivers close up from two levels. There is a central stage with continuous entertainment, except during the race of course! The winner's circle is also in the Neon garage on ground level and you will have an awesome view of all the celebrations if you are standing on the upper level.

The speedway plays host to the Nascar series, Indycar series and the Nascar Trucks, to name but a few. The speedway website **LVMS.com** is a good place to see what's taking place during your visit to Las Vegas, or maybe like us, you would prefer to organise your visit around something you want to see at the speedway.

For drag racing fans there is a drag strip at the speedway, simply named the Strip. There is also a smaller oval track called the Bullring.

If you want to get behind the wheel of a race car, you have two choices at the Speedway. **The Richard Petty Driving Experience** will give you the opportunity to drive a Nascar racer around the 1.5 mile oval, and the **Drive Exotics Ultimate Driving Experience** will give you the chance to drive one of your favourite supercars, such as a Ferrari or a Lamborghini, with several others to choose from, around a full-size racetrack inside the main oval. So get down there and burn some rubber.

The speedway is very easy to find, There are two ways to get there from the Strip. You can head north on the I-15 to exit 54, which is the Speedway Boulevard, or you can take the Las Vegas Boulevard, which is the road the Strip is on, and just head north past the Stratosphere Tower. You will see the speedway on your left hand side just after Nellis Boulevard. The checkered flag lane, also known as entrance number four, will take you to the ticketing building behind the main stand. The staff here are extremely helpful and there is also a great souvenir shop.

If you like aircraft, you can watch the military planes taking off and landing as **Nellis Air Force Base** is near the speedway.

The Hoover Dam
The Dam and the Memorial Bridge are free, but parking at the Dam is $7
35 Miles

No visit to Las Vegas would be complete without a trip to the Hoover Dam. Nestling between the rocks in Black Canyon, the Dam straddles the canyon walls and holds back the Colorado River to form **Lake Mead** behind it. Construction of the dam took five years and was completed in 1936.

The Dam was originally named Boulder Dam, but in 1947 it was renamed the Hoover Dam after America's 31st president, Herbert Hoover.

The Nevada-Arizona state line runs straight through the middle of the Dam, so at certain times of the year it can be one time on one side of the Dam and a different time on the other. If you stand on the state line, you can time travel by jumping from side to side across it as we did, but then we are a couple of big kids!

If you are going to drive to the Dam from the Strip, you should allow yourself an hour to get there. We have visited the Dam many times over the years and noticed the traffic going over it was getting very busy, but that has now been rectified by the opening of the new **Mike O'Callaghan–Pat Tillman Memorial Bridge**, which now takes all the through traffic away from the Dam and makes visiting much more enjoyable. The new bridge, which opened in October 2010, is an impressive arch structure and can be seen in all its glory from the dam itself.

The Hoover Dam

If you don't mind heights, take a walk on to the bridge and out to the centre. It makes for a great picture of the Dam and Lake Mead behind it, as the bridge towers high above the Dam and across the canyon. It looks massive and immovable, yet as we were standing on the apex of the bridge and taking pictures and a truck went past, the bridge gave what felt like a huge wobble. Time to walk back to solid ground.

You'll see the access to the bridge to your right on your drive down to the Dam, but my advice would be to visit it on the way back.

Parking is easy at the Dam. Turn left into the 'squeaky floor car park', as we call it for obvious reasons. It costs $7 to park (cash only) but after that you can walk out on to the Dam for free. There are tours several times daily and it can be accessed down the escalator at the visitor centre. Tours are very interesting and informative. You will be taken down into the workings of the dam to see the hydroelectric generators which are driven by the water flow to produce electricity.

Have a look around at all the mountains surrounding the Las Vegas valley until you see what look like some radio antennas - these are a

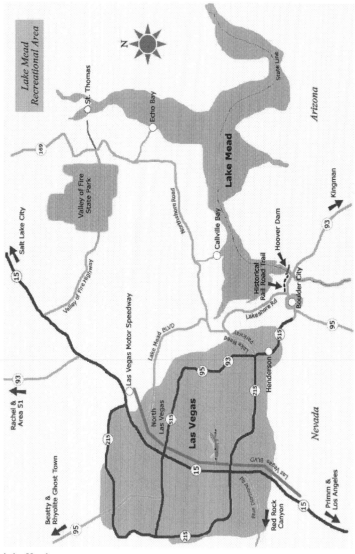

Lake Mead area map

good landmark to use until you learn your way around the valley and get your bearings. As you look towards these antennas you are facing east. You will pass just to the left of them through the mountains to reach the Hoover Dam. The route is relatively easy and hassle-free and an interesting drive.

Start off by following the strip south past Mandalay Bay. You will need to turn left soon, so keep to the left. Just past Sunset Road you will see a sign for car rental return to your left. Take this turning and then keep to the left after turning, and this will bring you on to the I-215 south. After a few miles you will need to turn on to the US-93/US-95 east to Boulder City. When you reach Boulder take the second light to the left and then follow this road to the Dam past the Hacienda Hotel.

There is a security checkpoint when approaching the dam and there is a small chance your vehicle could be searched. Just drop the window down, lift your sunglasses and smile and they should wave you through.

Hoover Dam Historical Rail Road Trail
30 Miles

Shortly after leaving the Memorial Bridge and heading back towards Las Vegas on the US-93, we spotted a Lake Mead scenic viewpoint to our right. Being the adventurous people we are, we had to go and have a look. From this elevated view point we could see one of the many Lake Mead marinas and the Boulder Basin section of the lake. We spotted an old disused train line and tunnel emerging out of the rock face to our left. We were very intrigued by this, as disused train lines and tunnels have always interested us and feel kind of spooky. We decided to see if we could get closer, so we got back on the US-93 and turned towards Lake Mead recreation area just past the Hacienda Hotel.

To our surprise we found a parking area only a short way down this road before we reached the fee pay zone that was signposted "Historical Hoover Dam Rail Road Trail". How lucky was that!

This old disused train trail was used to haul the materials and supplies needed to construct the dam between 1931, when construction began, and 1936, when it was completed, running 24 hours a day.

Hoover Dam historic railroad tunnel

There are five tunnels to explore along this section of the trail, all fairly close to each other. This is the only section still remaining of the 30-mile network of train tracks used for the dam.

Crews worked round the clock in three shifts for five months solid to complete the railroad. The tunnels were blasted out of the hard volcanic rock in temperatures of one hundred degrees and above.

Life was hard back then and the work was even harder. Many people left their homes and set up camp below in the Black Canyon to build the dam and create Lake Mead for our generation. The Black Canyon can be seen to our left as we walk along the trail towards the dam. All we can see today is water and the marina, but back then the whole area was a camp site for the workers and their families living in tattered wooden shelters, tents and cardboard boxes, with little food. The nearby Colorado River was used as their water supply. How times have changed.

You can explore this trail by bicycle or on foot. Dogs love it too, but the hairy four-legged ramblers just don't appreciate the scenery. The trail runs all the way back to the Hoover Dam parking lot, so make sure you have your drinking water, camera and hiking boots to hand. It will take around 40 minutes to reach the first tunnel, depending how fast you walk obviously. After that the rest of the tunnels are quite close together.

On the approach to the first tunnel, look to the right down the slope and you will see some huge concrete plugs. These were used to plug the holes in the dam before they installed the turbines. Keep your eyes open for bighorn sheep, ground squirrels, lizards and owls along the trail.

In 1977 this trail was used to film a sequence in a movie called The Gauntlet, starring Clint Eastwood and Sondra Locke. The sequence shows them on a Harley Davidson motorcycle being chased by a helicopter along the trail and through the tunnels. We had seen the movie many moons ago but didn't realise until we came home and watched it again that it was the place where we had just been walking.

Boulder City, Nevada
28 Miles

Boulder City is a quaint little town approximately twenty miles east of the glittering lights of Las Vegas and very close to the Hoover Dam. Built originally in the early 1930s to house the workers who were constructing the Hoover Dam (or Boulder Dam as it was known back then), it now has a population of only 1500 people.

When the exact site for the Dam became known, people hoping to work on the scheme began to settle and pitch camp next to the Colorado river, and the resulting collection of tents and cardboard boxes soon became known as Ragtown. The government decided to build a town to house these workers, so Boulder City was born.

Boulder City is one of only two places in Nevada where gambling is prohibited, the other being Panaca, north of Las Vegas close to the Utah border. So this quiet little town is a great place to visit if you want to escape the noise of the gambling machines in Las Vegas.

The traffic heading to and from the dam mostly bypasses the town, so it is quite a peaceful experience to stop and have a look round the many independent shops. There is a very interesting museum that explains how Boulder City evolved along with the dam. There are many places to eat and several motels. You will also find one or two very lush golf courses. We can never resist stopping here, even if it is only for an ice cream.

Returning to Las Vegas from Boulder City or the Hoover Dam will provide a great view of the whole of the Vegas valley, especially at night when it is lit up like a Christmas tree. Keep your eyes open after passing the Railroad Pass Hotel.

Death Valley
Death Valley National Park entrance fee $20 per vehicle
90 Miles

Death Valley National Park sits west of Las Vegas next to the Sierra Nevada mountains. This place is absolutely huge, covering over three million acres. The name makes it sound like somewhere you would never want to visit, but it is actually a very beautiful place, surrounded by mountains and stunning views fit for any artist's palette. The mountains help in maintaining the dry heat by causing the air pressure to increase at the valley floor, which is the lowest point in North America at 282 feet below sea level. The heat gets trapped as the higher pressure stops it escaping. Dry air also warms up more easily than humid air, hence the extreme temperatures in the summer months. The highest temperature recorded in Death Valley was at **Furnace Creek**, which we'll be visiting shortly - 134 degrees (56.7°C) in 1913, making Death Valley the second hottest place in the world, exceeded only by a record from Libya.

In this region there are wild flower displays, sand dunes that go on for miles, snow-covered mountain tops and lots of wildlife, if you're lucky enough to spot it. We did see a coyote once on the side of the road, not chasing roadrunners but begging for food from the passing cars. It was nice to see the little guy, even if he did look a bit scrawny.

Death Valley gets its name from the time of the California Gold Rush in 1849, when a group of people crossed here on their wagons and only a few made it through. A member of the party looked back and said 'Goodbye Death Valley' and the name stuck.

This place is vast. When you come here for the first time you will not realise how big it actually is, and you could miss out on some of its history and awesome scenery, as we did the first time we came. We found it daunting and confusing not knowing which roads to take and what we could be missing.

Let me tell you about some of the best viewing points and places of interest and give you a general idea of the geographical layout of this place, so that hopefully after reading this you will have some insight as to where you want to go and what you want to see when you get there.

There are several ways to enter Death Valley by road, but I am going to talk about the easiest and most direct route from Las Vegas. Heading south on Las Vegas Boulevard past Mandalay Bay, we turn right on to Blue Diamond Road, otherwise known as Highway 160. This road takes us all the way to Pahrump. Almost in the centre of Pahrump we turn left on to Highway 372. Just outside the city limits you enter California, and this road becomes highway 178. We continue through Shoshone and make a left on to Jubilee Pass Road, entering Death Valley National Park.

There is a sign here saying the next services are 72 miles away, so make sure you top up with gas before leaving Las Vegas. If you're short, go back and get some at Shoshone, because you'd need a bank loan to buy gas at Furnace Creek.

We will be picking up a map of Death Valley later from the visitor centre at Furnace Creek, and this road will take us straight there, so for now we are not worried about getting lost. The maps I have provided of the valley should serve you well from here on.

After a few miles we round a corner, and we can now see the valley floor stretched out in front of us for miles. It looks like hell on earth. What a sight as the white basin floor glimmers in the sunshine. We are now on Badwater Road, the Black Mountains to our right and the Panamint Mountains to our left. We are going to be driving up the east side of the valley against the Black Mountains.

To the left we pass the ruins of the old **Ashford Mill**. If you want to know the history of Death Valley and the story behind all the mining that was responsible for all the ruins scattered around the valley, then stopping off at the different ruins will tell the story. There are information plaques dotted around the sites.

Shortly after passing Ashford Mill we come to the West Side Road to our left. This dirt road is approximately forty miles long and will bring us back to Badwater Road much higher up. The road is very dry and dusty and can be a little bumpy in places, but when dry it is perfectly fine for ordinary two-wheel-drive family cars.

Check out the graves of Jimmy Dayton and Frank Shorty Harris just passed the Borax works. These guys were friends and respected pioneers in the area. Their story is a fascinating read. Jimmy Dayton died with his mules in the desert heat, close to the spot where he is now buried.

We decide to tackle the West Side Road on the way back heading south, so for now we continue north on Badwater Road. We have several miles to drive through this barren wilderness before we come to our first stop, which is the Badwater Basin, so we sit back and enjoy the scenery. This is where we saw Mr Coyote begging for food, so keep your eyes open for him and his relatives.

I strongly advise anyone doing this trip to stay on the tarmac roads or the dirt roads that take you on some of the scenic drives. You do not want to get lost in Death Valley. I will always remember something I saw on the local news in Las Vegas about a woman who went off the beaten track in Death Valley and her truck got stuck. She had driven over an animal burrow, and the bottom of the truck was beached. She was there for several days with her son and the family dog before the rangers found her. The woman and the dog survived, but unfortunately the son died. So stick to the hard surfaces, whether tarmac or dirt roads, and you will be fine.

Death Valley, Badwater Basin

By the time we arrive at **Badwater** the air conditioning in the truck is struggling to keep us cool. It is midday in September and the temperature outside has risen to almost 115 degrees. July and August are the hottest months here, as they are in Las Vegas, so if you come here during these months you can expect it to be even hotter.

Badwater Pool

Just to the left of the parking area there is a ticket machine where we pay our $20 fee to enter the park. Tickets can also be bought at the visitor centre in Furnace Creek and another ticket machine at Hells Gate. It doesn't really matter where you buy your ticket from, as long as you have one and display it in the car window.

Badwater is probably the best known and most visited place in Death Valley. This is the lowest point in North America. High up on the rocks next to the road is a sign indicating where sea level is – you can see it more easily by walking a little way out on to the salt flats.

The heat here is absolutely stifling and the air feels heavy due to the evaporation of the salty water from the Badwater pools. This makes walking around seem very labour intensive. We take some water and walk out a little way on to the salt flats - not too far though, we're not crazy. Just to stand there in that incredible heat and almost total silence is an unforgettable experience.

I think it is a good time to mention that there is a viewing point called **Dante's Peak**, almost immediately above us on top of the Black Mountains, over a mile higher in altitude. We will be heading there shortly to look down on where we are now.

Many years ago a surveyor mapping this area was disappointed that his mule would not drink from the pool, so he wrote 'bad water' on his map, hence the name. The salty pools here never dry up, and even contain fish that have evolved to live in these conditions. I can't begin to imagine what it must have been like to trek across this place on a mule in this heat. I take back every word I said earlier about the air conditioning in our truck struggling to keep us cool.

Can you believe they run a marathon out here called the Badwater Ultra Marathon? They even do it in the middle of July when the place is at its hottest. I think we will come here next year and set up a table next to the road selling energy drinks, we will make a fortune!

This pool began its life in the last ice age. Rain and snow runs down from the mountains hundreds of miles away in central Nevada, seeping out and emerging here at the Badwater Basin. Salts dissolve from old deposits and flow to the surface, making the spring water so unpalatable.

We continue along Badwater Road. It is 18 miles to Furnace Creek from here and I am tempted to ignore my own advice and do some off-roading on the way, as the terrain looks ideal to put this Jeep through its paces. But I decided against it as I don't want to get stuck or incur the wrath of a ranger if he happens to drive past while I am kicking up some dust. I should mention that in many of the national parks the rangers don't take kindly to anyone going off road and disrespecting the landscape without special permission.

There are a couple more interesting things to see along this road before we get to **Furnace Creek** in the centre of the valley. The first is the **Natural Bridge Canyon**. This is definitely worthwhile seeing. A short dirt road that is very rough in places takes us up to the parking area, and from here it is a half-mile walk slightly uphill to reach the large natural bridge that spans the canyon. Don't complain about the short uphill trek - just remember what I just said about the marathon. The bridge looks very unstable from underneath, but it is very impressive and makes a great picture.

The second is **Artist's Palette**. This is a scenic loop drive through volcanic rocks and sediment hills. The loop is nine miles long and starts and ends on Badwater Road. No vehicles over 25 feet long are allowed round the loop.

This place is very photogenic, especially in the afternoon as the light captures the rocky landscape perfectly. As we drive there are high rock formations both sides of the small road for most of the way – it's a bit like driving through a long, narrow canyon. This drive is also one way, and we emerge slightly further up on Badwater Road.

A few more miles along Badwater Road we come to a junction. To the right are **Zabriskie Point** and **Dante's Peak**, where we will be heading shortly, but for now we go left to the visitor centre just a mile down the road.

There are drinks and a water fountain at the visitor centre, so we make sure we top up our bottles for free at the fountain. As with any remote location, you will have to pay top dollar if you want to buy something to eat or drink, so bringing along plenty of food and drink with you in the truck or car in a cool bag is a very good idea. We have our cool bag in the back of the truck, spilling over with cool drinks we picked up from the supermarket before we left Las Vegas, so we are well prepared.

There is a hotel and a gas station at Furnace Creek, but we made sure we had plenty of gas when we left Vegas, because as I said earlier the gas prices here are sky high.

You will find the lowest golf course in the world at Furnace Creek - it can be seen just beyond the parking lot at the visitor centre. I can't imagine who would want to play golf in this heat.

We pick up some maps of the area, and I would strongly advise you to do the same. The rangers at the visitor centre are very helpful and eager to answer any questions, although they will want to see your park entrance ticket before they do so. It's a good idea to familiarise yourself with the area and find the places you want to visit on the local map of Death Valley. This way you won't get lost and it will save a whole heap of time. You could just use the maps I have provided as they are fairly complete, but the official Death Valley map will have some additional information about different places.

So we turn right out of the visitor centre and head back the way we came. We are now heading for Zabriskie Point and Dante's Peak, both of which have lent their names to Hollywood films. These two viewing points, especially Dante's Peak, are on top of the Black Mountains, which overlook the Death Valley basin floor and give an awesome panoramic view of the whole of the Badwater Basin below, where we have just been driving.

A few miles past the junction with Badwater Road, where we came from earlier, we reach **Zabriskie Point**. Parts of the 1970 movie of the same name were shot here. The gullies and mud hills resemble sand dunes on the edge of the Black Mountains. In the distance we can see the flat salty basin floor. There are some hiking trails that take you out into the dunes and beyond which give a better overall view of the valley below - details of all the trails can be found on the official Death Valley map.

Dante's Peak, or **Dante's View** as it is sometimes known, is where we are heading next, and this is the one we are most looking forward to seeing. Leaving Zabriskie Point we turn right, and after a few miles we see Dante's View Road on the right. This road is 13 miles long and will take us all the way to the top. The road starts off fairly flat, but when we get closer to the top it gets extremely steep. The last quarter mile is a 15 per cent grade, so no trailers or large camper vans are allowed at the top. There is a small parking area just before the last quarter mile, so if you have a large vehicle or don't like the idea of the steep grade you can leave the vehicle here and continue on foot.

View from Dante's Peak

The summit of Dante's Peak is 5700 feet high, and we can see some fantastic views of the whole of the southern part of the national park. The salty basin floor is shimmering in the sunshine more than a mile below us. The Panamint Mountains on the other side of the valley fade into the heat haze.

Standing on the edge of the cliffs here is slightly scary, but it's a stunning experience. Be careful close to the edge and away from the paved area, as there are no barriers and the rocks are very loose in places and not safe for everyone.

From the parking area looking out this is known as Dante's View. Over to the left there is a short path which takes us to the actual summit of Dante's Peak. I cannot even begin to describe the awesome views that can be experienced from here, so get on the next plane and come see for yourself!

Looking down we can see the Badwater Road we drove along earlier snaking its way along the side of the valley. It looks like a thick black line, and if there are any cars they are difficult to spot, as it's well over a mile straight down to the valley floor from here. If we stand in the right place we can just about see Badwater immediately below us, where we walked out on to the salt flats a couple of hours ago.

After leaving Dante's Peak we head back past the visitor centre towards the north end of the valley.

You may have heard about the mysterious moving rocks of Death Valley. These rocks, some of which weigh several hundred pounds, have featured in many documentaries. Scientists still cannot explain why they slide across the valley floor, leaving long trails behind them in the sediment. There are several possible explanations, but the mystery remains, because no one has ever actually seen them move. The valley floor is almost perfectly flat and almost always dry and covered with mud cracks.

These rocks can be found at a place called **Racetrack Valley**, or **Racetrack Playa** as it is sometimes known (a playa is a dry lake bed). It is awkward to get there as it is in a fairly remote location. If you ask a ranger where it is or how to reach it, they will probably try to talk you out of going there. But don't be put off, as it's a fascinating place.

Racetrack Valley is located at the north end of Death Valley and there is only one way to get there (there is another way, but as it involves some serious off-roading I wouldn't recommend it unless you know the area very well).

We carry on past the visitor centre on Highway 190 until we come to Scotty's Castle Road on our right. We need to turn here to reach Racetrack Playa.

Sand dunes, Highway 190

Highway 190 carries on to the sand dunes just a few miles down the road. These dunes are comparable with what you might find in the Sahara Desert, and they stretch for miles across the valley. Then it's on to **Stovepipe Wells**, a tiny little place with a gas station, a motel and not much else, except some very cheap ice cream, less than a dollar in fact. I can never resist ice cream, especially when it's that cheap.

Finally the road leaves Death Valley and heads west to Lone Pine.

About forty miles along Scotty's Castle Road we come to **Ubehebe Crater**. This massive hole in the ground was formed two thousand years ago by a volcanic eruption which spilled molten rock and lava up to six miles away, leaving behind a crater 500 feet deep and half a mile across.

To get to the Racetrack we need to take Racetrack Valley Road from this crater. The racetrack is 27 miles down this unpaved dirt road. I recommend a four-wheel drive vehicle for this, not because a car would get stuck but for the extra clearance it will give underneath, as the road can get rough and has some high points in places. We did see some cars along this road coping very well, but the choice is yours - I don't recommend it for cars.

Teakettle Junction is a small junction on this remote dirt road. Located six miles from the Racetrack, it has a signpost famous for being covered in kettles contributed by passing visitors. It makes for quite a sight. You wonder what came first - the name or the kettles.

We came here to the Racetrack on our second trip to Death Valley. We wanted to make sure we had enough time during daylight to get here and back and spend some time exploring the Racetrack and the rocks.

Camping is allowed at the Racetrack for tents and RVs, but there is little else here apart from the famous moving rocks. Though as I said, no one has ever actually seen them move! It's also advisable to bring plenty of water and some food.

It would probably be asking too much to cram all this into just one day's trip to Death Valley, but the southern end of the valley, which includes the Badwater Drive, Zabriskie Point, Dante's Peak and the visitor centre can easily be seen in a day.

There is a small motel at Stovepipe Wells, so if you wanted to see everything without returning to Las Vegas and coming back again the next day, an option would be to stay here for the night after exploring the southern end of the valley, then continue up to the Ubehebe Crater and Racetrack Playa the following morning.

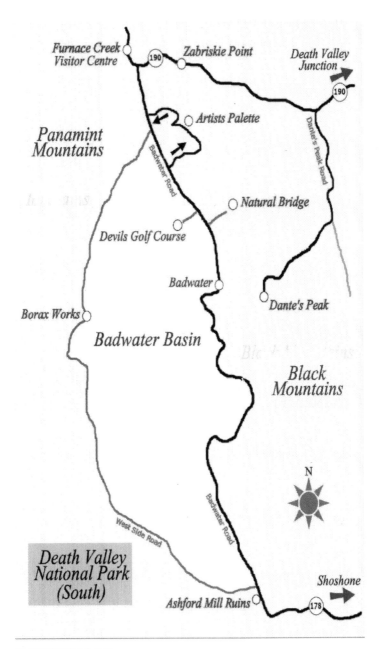

Death Valley South map

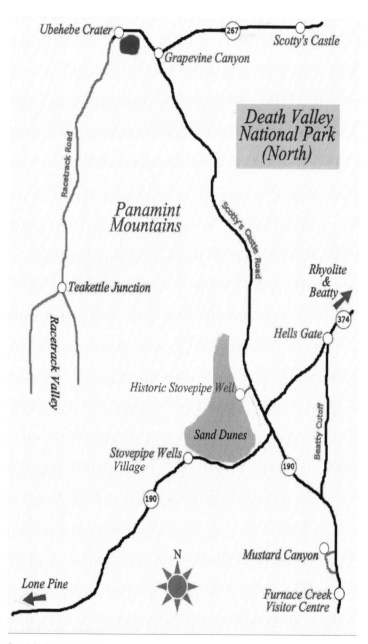

Death Valley North map

St Thomas Ghost Town

Lake Mead National Park - entrance fee $10 per vehicle for 7 days
65 Miles

St Thomas started out as a pioneering settlement in 1865 and grew to be a large town. The residents here enjoyed a quiet life until the construction of the Hoover Dam began, when they knew their town and their lifestyle were doomed.

Shortly after the completion of the Dam in 1936, the rising waters of the Colorado River slowly formed Lake Mead and flooded the town of St Thomas. The last person to leave, in June 1938, was a guy named Hugh Lord. He waited until the waters were lapping at his door, then jumped into a boat and rowed away from his doomed house.

After all these years St Thomas has risen again, as the waters of Lake Mead have slowly been falling due to increasing demand from the surrounding area. There isn't a great deal left of St Thomas after all this time under water, but there are still some ruins and some reminders of what life must have been like scattered around the valley floor. We are both lovers of ghost towns and this place feels a little different to others we have visited - maybe because it's the only one we have seen that has spent the past 70 years under water - but it was certainly very interesting and had an eerie feeling to it.

I would highly recommend a visit to St Thomas if you are interested in the history of the area. There are some artefacts scattered around the valley floor here and there, but please don't disturb or take anything, as this will just spoil the experience for other people. It is illegal to remove historic artefacts.

The two-and-a-half-mile walk around the valley is marked out by trail signs, so bring some good walking shoes and some water, especially if the weather is hot. The trail is not maintained, so be careful. We always carry a mobile phone with us just in case something should happen, as some of the places we visit are quite remote.To get to St Thomas from the Strip is about a 65-mile drive, and there are two options. The first is a picturesque drive along the side of Lake Mead. Drive south past Mandalay Bay and take a left on to the 215 just past the airport. Keep going on this road and it will eventually turn into Lake Mead Parkway. Keep going past Lake Las Vegas hotel on your left and you will come to a pay station. There is a fee for the Lake Mead National Park, but it is valid for seven days, so you can come back through any time.

This is a good time to ask the ranger at the kiosk if the dirt road that leads down to St Thomas is open, as sometimes when the level of Lake Mead rises after higher than normal rainfall the valley of St Thomas gets flooded and they close the road. If the ranger says the road is closed and you don't want to see anything else in the park, you can turn around and pay your money another time when the road is open.

Immediately after the pay station turn left on to North Shore road. This road will take you all the way to the dirt road leading to St Thomas. There are many places to stop off on the way and it is a lovely drive, though in parts remote. Unfortunately the lake is not visible along North Shore Road, but there are several turnings to your right along the way that will take you down to bay areas and small towns next to the lake.

You won't see any signs for St Thomas until you get to the dirt road to your right, immediately before a pay station for people entering the park from the opposite direction. The dirt road is four miles long and is OK for cars as well as trucks.

The second route to St Thomas will take you through the Valley of Fire, another great place to visit which I will talk about next. If you want to visit both these places in a day it can be done easily, if you start out at a reasonable time in the morning. Remember that the gate to the dirt road down to St Thomas is only open dawn to dusk. My suggestion would be to visit the Valley of Fire first in the morning and then head down to St Thomas in the afternoon. If you follow my directions in the next section you will exit the Valley of Fire on the east side, right next to the dirt road that leads down to St Thomas. You could always do it in the opposite direction too and visit St Thomas first - the choice is yours and either way is good.

Valley of Fire
Valley of Fire State Park, entrance fee $10 per vehicle
56 Miles

To reach the Valley of Fire, which is about 56 miles north east of Las Vegas, head north on the I-15 towards Mesquite and Salt Lake City and take exit 75 on to the Valley of Fire Highway. Here at the exit you will find a casino, a gas station and even a smoke shop if you need to stock up on cigarettes. Once in the mountains you will come to the entrance to the Valley of Fire State Park, where there is another fee - just a few dollars, but these places do have to be maintained and preserved, and when you consider how long you can spend inside some of these fantastic parks admiring the breathtaking scenery, it can be considered a cheap day out.

The Valley of Fire is named after the red sandstone formations formed from the shifting sand dunes 150 million years ago, back in the age of the dinosaurs. Basket makers and the Anasazi people lived here, but their stay would have been short due to the scarcity of water in the area. Fine examples of rock art have been left behind by these ancient people and can be found at several sites within the park.

There are plenty of RV hookups and camping areas with shower facilities and restrooms for those who wish to stay a few days in the Valley of Fire. There are picnic areas and BBQ tables at almost every vista, so enjoy and have fun as we did.

Let's assume you entered the Valley of Fire from the I-15. A little way down the road, after paying your money at the pay station and before you reach the visitor centre, you will find a two-mile scenic route loop road which provides some of the valley's most scenic and interesting rock formations, such as the **Arch Rock** and the **Piano Rock** formations.

The visitor centre is open daily except for Christmas Day and is a very good source of information about the area and the rock formations. Take some drinks with you, as the temperatures can reach 120 degrees on the hotter days in the high summer months of July and August. As I said before, we always carry a small foldaway cool bag in the back of the truck full of drinks. Nearly all the hotels have ice machines, and with the ice in the cool bag the drinks stay cold all day even after the ice has melted.

We head north from the visitor centre to see **Mouse's Tank**, named after a renegade who used the area as a hideout in the 1890s. This is a natural basin in the rock where water collects after rainfall. The half-mile hike to Mouse's Tank is like stepping into a cowboy movie, with meandering trails and some very interesting rock formations. The atmosphere is wonderful - so quiet and relaxing. Most of the hike is sandy, with the odd rocky surface.

Heading further north into the Valley of Fire, we come to **Rainbow Vista** and its panoramic views of the multi-coloured red sandstone. Then on to the **Fire Canyon** and **Silica Dome**. Here you will have an excellent view of the deep red sandstone in the Fire Canyon and stunning views of the unique geological features of the Silica Dome.

A little further north are **Duck Rock** and the **White Domes**. This is another trail to explore, with more stunning formations of brilliant contrasting colours, a picnic area and a one-mile scenic trail with fabulous views. You will have to double back now, as you have seen all there is to explore here, and head back towards the visitor centre. You can top up with water at the centre if it is still open.

Valley of Fire – Seven Sisters Rocks

Heading east from the visitor centre you will come to the **Seven Sisters**, a fascinating formation of seven red rocks. It is situated by the roadside, with yet another picnic area. A little further down the road are the **Cabins**, which were built from native sandstone in the 1930s as shelter for passing travellers by the CCC (Civilian Conservation Corps). Either of these two vistas is a perfect place for a relaxing stop during your visit to the Valley of Fire.

Along the roadside you will see some petrified logs. These were washed into the area from an ancient forest some 225 million years ago. The last viewing point in the valley is the **Arrowhead Trail**, which takes you to **Elephant Rock**, a huge structure resembling an elephant which is quite a sight.

A little way down the road you will come to US 169, the road I was talking about earlier from Las Vegas to St Thomas. Immediately in front of you, you will see the dirt road leading down to St Thomas. If you don't want to pay another fee to enter Lake Mead National Park or see St Thomas, then turn around and return to Vegas the way you came. Another option if you don't want to cover the same ground is to turn left and head north to **Overton** and **Longdale**, where you will find the most stunning ranches with little white picket fences just like in the movies. You will also find a gas station here. This route will take you back on to the I-15 a little further north from where you came into the valley earlier.

The Grand Canyon
Grand Canyon National Park entrance fee $25 per vehicle

West Rim 120 Miles | North Rim 270 Miles | South Rim 280 Miles

One of the most popular excursions from Las Vegas is the Grand Canyon. The fantastic views and the helpless feeling you get when standing on the edge of a mile-deep hole are second to none. You may have already caught sight of it if you flew into Vegas from the east, but seeing it from the ground and being able to stand on the edge and even do some hiking down into the canyon is a must for any adventurous tourist.

There are several ways you can visit the Grand Canyon, but we like to do it by car. It's a lovely drive and the weather should also be good in the summer months, although occasionally when we have been there at the canyon edge it has been a little chilly, so to be on the safe side we always throw a sweater or hooded top in the back of the truck. You can always buy a top there if you forget.

Don't forget your supplies of cold drinks and munchies for the journey, as I mentioned before. It is always a good idea to have something to eat and drink in the back of the truck, especially when it's hot. The small cool bag we use we bought from one of the supermarkets for $8, and it's ideal. Just throw in some ice in the morning from the ice machine when you leave your hotel, and even after it has turned to water the drinks still keep nice and cool. It flattens down when not in use, so it fits nicely into the suitcase.

If you prefer to fly over the canyon, you can book a trip either on the strip or from your hotel (almost all the hotels in Las Vegas have a desk where you can book all sorts of trips and shows). Helicopter trips are leaving all the time from McCarran Airport, and again they can be booked from your hotel. If you wish to fly over the canyon, then our advice would be to book your trip after you arrive here in Las Vegas, as this is normally the cheapest option. However, we prefer to drive, so that's what I am going to concentrate on here.

The Grand Canyon is on an Indian reservation, so be respectful at all times and make sure you take your litter home with you. We should all do this all the time anyway! The canyon lies within the Grand Canyon National Park and whatever direction you enter from you will have to pay a fee. The fee here is $25 per vehicle, and the pass will last for seven days.

If you are going to visit several national parks during your stay, it may be worth talking to the ranger at the kiosk and paying a little more for a pass that will give you access to several national parks. It will save you some money.

There are several places you can head for to see the canyon. The **West Rim** is the closest to Las Vegas at around 120 miles. If you dare, you can walk out on to the **Sky Walk**, a horseshoe-shaped shell of glass that suspends us nervous wrecks over the canyon edge. They made us put some very trendy covers over our shoes so as not to scratch the glass. Unless the rules have changed you are not allowed to take cameras on to the Sky Walk - they say this is because if you drop a camera it will scratch the glass floor, but being cynical I think there may be a financial reason – they want to sell us their own photographs! Until this changes you can always take pictures from the edge. I may sound so tight that I squeak when I walk, but at least I am not going to get ripped off and I don't want you to be. I don't mind spending money as long as I am getting value for it.

There is also a coach trip that goes to the West Rim, but if you have already rented a car you won't need a coach.

The **North Rim** of the Grand Canyon is a little more remote – it's around 270 miles from Las Vegas, but well worth the extra mileage. The approach is shrouded in forest and makes a lovely drive among lots of wildlife.

Log cabin, Grand Canyon North Rim

When we went there we didn't realise that the lodge hotel was so close to the edge. After checking in and getting the keys to our log cabin, I walked over to a huge window where several people were gazing out, wondering what all the fuss was about. I looked out and had such a shock that my knees started to knock together. I was peering right into the canyon for the first time.

That trip to the North Rim was our very first visit to the Grand Canyon, so I was catching flies for a few minutes staring at this enormous hole before me!

The **South Rim** is by far the most popular with tourists. It lies around 280 miles from Las Vegas. Ninety per cent of people who visit the Grand Canyon come here, so naturally it's a lot busier, with more shops and an abundance of hiking trails.

Grand Canyon South Rim

I strongly advise a stop-off in **Williams**, Arizona, on the way. Williams is a small town, known as the gateway to the Grand Canyon. You will find many motels here, the locals are friendly and there are several places to get something to eat and gas up. Williams is on the old Route 66 mother road, which has long been broken up since the introduction of interstates, so keep your eyes open for memorabilia.

Now you have some choices. You can drive up to the canyon from Williams, which is around 60 miles. You will notice when you leave Williams that the trees and the shrubbery slowly disappear and it becomes quite barren. Then as you get closer to the canyon the trees and shrubs slowly appear again, bigger ones this time.

Grand Canyon train

The other choice is to take the **Grand Canyon Train**. You will find the station in Williams, and tickets can be booked in advance or just bought on the day, as we did. It's a great ride through the wilderness at a relatively slow speed and arrives very close to the canyon rim. The train takes around two hours each way. Walk up some steps and you're more or less on the edge.

The only downside to the train is that on its return it leaves at a set time, so if you are not aboard you will have to walk or hitch a lift back to Williams. I suggest that if you are planning to go exploring or hiking when at the canyon rim, you should take the car. That way you can return whenever you are ready. During the return journey on the train be ready for a surprise, but I won't spoil it and tell you what it is!

One time on a visit to the Grand Canyon we took some friends who had not seen it before. I drove from Las Vegas to the South Rim and back in one day, and it was a long one. So I would suggest breaking the journey and spending the night in Williams.

To drive to the West Rim of the Grand Canyon we need to head past the Hoover Dam and over the new memorial bridge, using the directions I gave in my section on the Hoover Dam. Continue along the US-93 and turn left on to County Highway 25 towards Dolan Springs. Quite a few miles along this road the West Rim is signposted to the right. The rest of the journey is along a dirt road. The good news is that this road is fairly flat and perfectly fine for most cars, apart from the dust it kicks up.

For the North Rim, we need to head north on the I-15. At the town of St. George we turn right on to Highway 9. When we reach Hurricane, we pick up UT-59 and head south to Colorado City. Here the road turns into the AZ-389.

At Fredonia we turn right on to the US-89a to Jacob Lake, where we turn right again on to US-67. We are now on the Grand Canyon Highway. This road will take us all the way to the rim of the Grand Canyon, but be aware that it is closed during the winter months. **The South Rim** is a little more straightforward. First head east on US-93 past the Hoover Dam and on to Kingman. Here we pick up the I-40 east towards Flagstaff. Now sit back and enjoy the view – it's 112 miles to Williams on this road. In Williams we need to take the US-64 all the way to the South Rim

Meteor Crater
Admission fee: adults $15, children 6-17 $8, under fives free.
294 Miles

Arizona Meteor Crater

The famous Meteor Crater, one of the best-preserved and most spectacular on Earth, is located fairly close to the Grand Canyon and Williams. If you want to visit it I would suggest doing so while you are in the area visiting the Grand Canyon.

The crater is almost a mile wide and over 500 feet deep. It was created 50,000 years ago by a meteorite measuring 150 feet across and travelling at 26,000 miles per hour. It must have been an almighty

71

bang! Fortunately there were no humans living in the area back then, but the wildlife must have had a nasty shock.

On the edge of the crater steel walkways and viewing points have been constructed, and these are ideal for taking pictures. I gave up trying to capture all of this enormous hole in one shot - the only way to do this effectively is from the air. Unfortunately walking down to the centre of the crater is not allowed, but you can join a guided hiking group down into the crater for a fee.

There is also a place to get something to eat and drink here, but **no gas!**

Two Guns Ghost Town
285 Miles

On the way to the Meteor Crater, just off the I-40, there is a small ghost town called Two Guns. You will see it to your right as you drive east towards the crater. If you like ghost towns, Two Guns is definitely worth a look. There is very easy access from the I-40 at exit 230.

Two Guns ghost town

There are many old buildings scattered around, including an old zoo. The sign on the front saying 'Mountain Lions' is still intact, and some of the old cages to the rear are still visible.

I would advise you take great care while looking around the scattered buildings, as they are becoming very unsafe. It looks as though many years ago a river flowed through the town and some of the unsafe buildings are perched on the side of this old dry river bed.

Area 51 and Rachel
151 miles

Hidden in the mountains to the north of Las Vegas is the infamous Area 51, also known as Groom Lake or Dreamland. There is a top-secret US government installation here which they still deny exists to this day, though it can be seen on satellite photos. UFO buffs will know the place I am talking about, along with the small town called Rachel, where the **"Little Ale'Inn"** can be found.

If you don't already know about Area 51, I will just say that there is no chance of gaining access and going inside to have a look round. What attracts people to the area is the mystery and denial that has gone side by side with the base for many years.

I have always loved a good mystery, or anything that can't be explained, and this place does it for me. With all the talk about captured aliens and alien spacecraft associated with Area 51, it has become a great tourist attraction. Although there might not really be any aliens or flying saucers, it's the fact that it has been kept so secret that makes this place so intriguing. The desolate location, hidden behind several mountain ranges and miles from anywhere, also makes it that bit more intriguing. I know it won't appeal to everyone, so I won't go on for too long, but no book about places of interest around Las Vegas would be complete without a mention of this place.

Don't go thinking that when you get up near to Area 51 you will find people and UFO watchers everywhere, because in all the times we have been there we have seen hardly anyone. It's miles from anywhere and you will only see the odd car now and again, and maybe a cow or two. When you are near Groom Lake Road, which is one of two main entrances to Area 51 along the Extra Terrestrial Highway, you are actually only a little over 20 miles from Rachel, but it will feel like you are hundreds of miles from anywhere. It can be very spooky, especially at night, so if you are going to be freaked out then make sure you go during the day.

If you do want to head up to Area 51 its roughly a three-hour drive each way, but in my opinion it's worth every minute.

Here's the route. You need to leave Las Vegas and head north on the I-15 towards St George and Salt Lake City. The traffic will soon thin out and the scenery starts to become very open. Now you are on roads where you will be able to see for miles, so relax and enjoy the scenery.

After a few minutes you will see the **Las Vegas Motor Speedway** on your right. I have been to see the Indycars race here twice, and it was an awesome experience. If you like motor sport, check out what's on before you leave home.

Area 51 - the road to Rachel

Now take exit 64, which is the US-93 North, the Great Basin Highway. You'll see the road stretching out in front of you for miles. Get used to this as you will see many long roads like this one, they seem to be everywhere in Nevada. Just when you think you have seen the mother of all roads stretching out to the horizon, along comes an even longer one. **Ash Springs** will be your last chance to get fuel, so if you're running low get it here - there is nothing else before Rachel. Actually there is no gas station at Rachel either, but the people who run the Little Ale'Inn carry some gas out back for emergencies. It will however cost you a lot more than at the gas station.

Area 51 - ET Highway sign

Shortly after you leave Ash Springs make a left on to NV-318 and almost immediately you will see a fork in the road - you need to go left. You are now on **Extra Terrestrial Highway 375**. Be sure to pull over and take a picture at the picnic area next to the big Extra Terrestrial Highway sign.

Now you are only around 20 miles or so from Area 51. You will see some open range signs that warn you about the cattle that wander on to the roads, so be careful not to connect with one, or you may have a rather large dent in the front of the car, especially at night when they are much harder to spot and seem to enjoy playing chicken with the car headlights!

When you pass over the next mountain range, which is called **Hancock Summit,** look over to your left when you reach the other side and you will see a very long dirt road heading off into the mountains to your left. This is Groom Lake Road, and it leads straight to one of the main gates of Area 51, 13 miles up this road.

Groom Lake Road

There are two entrances to Area 51 on Extra Terrestrial Highway. This is the south entrance, while the other is further up the road towards Rachel and less well known. The road is not marked and there are no signs, so it can easily be missed if you don't know what to look for, as we did the first time we came here. This road is actually designed to be dusty. It has a special surface that kicks up the maximum amount of dust when a vehicle passes through, so that the security at the base can monitor any traffic going up and down it.

Be very careful if you decide to head up this road, as you are being watched. You are not breaking any laws, but the line between where public land ends and government land begins is very grey.

If you decide to drive up this road, you won't actually get to see the main gate or gate house, but you will see some warning signs and some orange posts either side of the road before you reach the main gate. **DO NOT GO ANY FURTHER**. If you cross over this point, the security guards (known as the Cammo Dudes), who are probably already watching you in their truck from high up on the mound to the right, will swoop down and put a gun to your head. You will then be arrested by the local sheriff and charged with trespassing. This won't look good on your visa the next time you want to visit America!

We only ventured about halfway up this road, as I wasn't going to risk getting arrested and fined and not being able to visit the States again. Besides, it is very spooky, especially at night.

About eight miles up Groom Lake Road on the right there is a pull-off area - this is where people go camping and UFO spotting. It's an ideal place to spot the Cammo Dudes if you don't want to drive right up to the main entrance where the warning signs are and risk getting swooped upon. From the top of the high mound here you can look over towards the main entrance and the roads the Dudes use to patrol the area. Be aware that if you do stop here the Dudes may try to frighten you off by driving up close to where you are. Don't worry too much as you are still on public land and not breaking any laws.

The Black Mailbox

If you keep driving past Groom Lake Road you will come across the famous **Black Mailbox** about five miles up the road on the left. It's not actually black any more, as it has been painted white. There are rumours that it used to be the mailbox for Area 51, but I can't imagine a top secret US military base shrouded in mystery and the subject of many documentaries having its mail delivered by Postman Pat. It now belongs to a local rancher.

The dirt road you can see next to the mailbox leads to Groom Lake Road about four miles up. This is a another favourite place for UFO watchers, and if you are here at midnight you might encounter a coachload of tourists hoping to see some strange lights over the mountains. More often than not the lights do indeed appear. It's a must see, but whether they are alien UFOs or not is a subject for another book! About ten miles past the mailbox you will find the small town of **Rachel**,

77

and when I say small I mean tiny. It consists of trailer homes and not much else. The only thing to see here is the famous **Little Ale'Inn**, which has been featured in many UFO and Area 51 documentaries. The first time we came here there was a small gas station with one pump, but this has now long gone. It's an ideal place to stop off for some refreshment. The staff have always been friendly towards us and the food is good - I recommend the blueberry pie, which is delicious. You can buy alien memorabilia, and they will rent you a trailer if you want to stay the night. This could be a useful idea if you are planning to head up to the Black Mailbox at midnight for some UFO spotting.

Area 51 - Rachel sign

If you head north from Rachel towards Tonopah, you will come across **Warm Springs**, which is on the junction at the end of ET Highway 375 and is around 60 miles north of Rachel. It has been mentioned on several websites as being a ghost town, but there's not much to see here now. If it used to be a town, most of it has now gone, with just a couple of old buildings left standing. When we were there they had put fences up so we couldn't even explore the buildings, which is what it's all about for us. But if you're passing it's worth a look.

Rhyolite Ghost Town
Completely free
127 Miles

It always fascinates us to visit a ghost town, looking at the deserted streets and thinking how these places were once heaving with people going about their daily business. Now the people and their businesses are almost forgotten and all that remains is some dusty old run-down ruins to remember them by. I love to stand in the middle of a ghost town and imagine going back in time, to see exactly what was happening in the spot where I am standing. Maybe it's all happening at the same time, and I am just seeing it from a different page in the multi-universe book.

The people who lived in these towns had their day-to-day problems, just as we do today, but now they are all long forgotten. I sometimes sit back at home when something is stressing me out and reflect that in a hundred years' time nobody is going to give a damn. It can help!

If you like ghost towns as much as we do, you can find an abundance of old towns and ruins dotted around Nevada, Arizona, Utah and California. I am only going to talk about a couple of them in this book, but if you want to explore more there are many books with detailed information about all these towns, or you can look on the internet. There are many websites dedicated to ghost towns in the USA, and they are very interesting and informative. One such website is **ghosttowns.com**, which lists every ghost town in the USA with detailed information and pictures.

Rhyolite is within fairly easy reach of Las Vegas. It is probably one of the best known ghost towns, and will definitely whet your appetite for visiting more of them the next time you come.

A real ghost town is a completely deserted old town with several buildings left standing, or at least some substantial ruins that you can investigate and imagine what it must have been like to live there. A ghost town to me is not a town that is still inhabited, or one which has been commercialised with lots of gift shops, and where the old saloon where weary cowboys once stopped off for a whisky is now a trendy restaurant. One such place in my opinion is Calico in California, a great old town with lots of stories to tell, but very commercialised.

Rhyolite is my favourite ghost town by far. Its around 127 miles north west of Las Vegas through open wilderness. Heading north, take exit 42a off the I-15 and head up the US-95 Memorial Highway. You will pass through Indian Springs and Amargosa Valley on the way. The US-95 will take you all the way to **Beatty**, another quaint little town with a couple of gas stations. With gas stations come bathrooms, and you will probably be needing one by now.

When you arrive in Beatty you will come to a crossroads. You are not far away now. Rhyolite is around twenty minutes away to your left, but the gas station is to your right, so you may want to call there first, then double back.

Just before Beatty on the US-95 you will see some ruins over to your right. This is the remains of a place called Carrara. They are what is left of an old marble mine, active around the turn of the 19th century. The mine produced lots of good quality marble, but transporting it was a big headache. Production stopped because it was almost impossible to transport the marble back then and keep it in one piece, and the mine closed.

You can drive up the dirt road to the buildings which are left standing. The actual mine is obviously much further up on the hillside, but we didn't venture that far. The buildings are kind of strange. We couldn't really figure out what they were supposed to be, especially the perfect circles in some of the smaller buildings. It's very quiet and peaceful and you can see for miles, so Carrera is definitely worth a short stop. I should also mention here, that unlike in the national parks, these wide open spaces are public land and you are free to drive anywhere you want without breaking any laws.

When arriving at Rhyolite you will see some weird art displayed on your left as you drive up. We have no idea why they have done this, as it seems totally inappropriate to be displaying art next to a ghost town, but who are we to question their reasons?

You will also see a small hut to your left. Sometimes you will find an elderly couple here who know all the history of the town and the surrounding area. They are very interesting to talk to and have some very informative leaflets about the town. They are not always around, as sometimes it's just way too hot!

Once again, remember to bring some drinks and a cool bag with you, because you are now on the edge of Death Valley and temperatures here can get extremely hot in the summer months.

Old bank building, Rhyolite ghost town

Further up the track you will find the main part of the town. There are some old bank buildings and an old school to your left, a hardware store to your right and the railway station right at the very top. The old rail tracks have long gone, but you can still see where they used to go. This whole area is also known as the Bullfrog mining district.

If you drive down the dusty road opposite the old bank buildings you will find the jail. It's still remarkably intact, with the bars still in the windows. Behind the jail on the side of the hill you will see the old mineshaft, which is fenced off as it is dangerous to go down inside.

However you can still climb up and have a look inside. From the mineshaft there is an awesome view of the town. We took a photo from here and we managed to find an old photograph on the internet from 1911 to compare it against. It shows the streets and buildings and even the jailhouse in the foreground, with several people going about their business. It was an awesome feeling to be standing where that picture was taken back in 1911.

There is also a 'bottle house' made entirely from old beer bottles. Sometimes this is fenced off as it had to be restored, so they obviously feel the need to try to preserve their work from people who have no respect and want to damage it.

Rhyolite ghost town from the mine

When you head back down towards the highway from the town, there is an old cemetery over to your right down a small dusty road. The cemetery is full of former residents of the town, including Mary Elizabeth Madison, better known as Panniment Annie. Born in 1910 and famous in the area for being very independent, her story is a fascinating read. She died from cancer in 1979 and was buried here in Rhyolite cemetery. The dusty road will also bring you back to the main highway.

If you make a right when you get back to the main highway 374, it will take you into **Death Valley**. There are several routes into Death Valley - this one will bring you through the daylight pass to **Hell's Gate**.

Route 66

140 Miles to Ludlow California
178 Miles to Seligman Arizona

The historic Route 66 runs from Chicago to Los Angeles. The original road is now broken up into different sections, due mainly to the introduction of the interstate. Not many people who come here to Las Vegas realise that one of the biggest sections of this nostalgic road still left fairly intact is within easy driving distance of Las Vegas.

Las Vegas is in the state of Nevada, and the border of California is less than forty miles away at Primm. The section of the mother road I am talking about runs from **Ludlow** in California to **Seligman** in Arizona. We decided to spend two days exploring this unspoilt and sometimes barren road, spending the night in Kingman, Arizona.

To reach Route 66 at Ludlow takes about two hours from Las Vegas. The interstate takes you all the way to Ludlow and would be the quickest route, but we prefer to use the smaller roads when we can, as they are much more interesting and have less traffic.

The drive down to Route 66 is almost as interesting as the road itself. After filling up with gas we head south on the I-15 and turn left at exit 286 shortly after passing Primm, on to Nipton Road towards Nipton. Now a vast dusty expanse has opened up in front of us, just the way we like it. Using the map we make our way down to Ludlow. For the last few miles we have to hop on to the I-40, but it's not far. Exit 50 is the one we want for Ludlow. Under the bridge and turn left and we are now on Route 66 pointing east.

 This section of Route 66 is also known as National Trails Highway. There is a large truck parking area here, so we pull over to get some sun on our faces and make some coffee from our travel kettle. What a good buy that thing was.

We check out the old deserted Ludlow café and gas station, along with some spooky old buildings just down the road. Just as well we have our kettle - it's been a while since they brewed any coffee here.

From here this lonely desert road becomes very desolate, even harsh in places, all the way to Needles on the Arizona border. From Ludlow we continue on towards Amboy. The Mojave desert is looking pretty barren and civilisation seems a million miles away. The Santa Fe Railroad runs alongside the road and crosses over from time to time, and it's a great opportunity to take some pictures of these endless trains that trundle slowly across the desert. Some look as if they are a mile long, with several engines pulling and pushing at both ends. We tried, but we couldn't tempt the driver to sound the horn as he was passing, maybe he is sick of tourists waving and taking pictures of him at work.

We noticed on the map that there is a town called **Bagdad**, but we couldn't even see any ruins where it was supposed to be. Later, the guy who runs the gas station at Amboy told us that it's the authorities' policy in the county to make sure all ruins are removed. I mentioned the ruins of the old café and gas station which had been left at Ludlow, but he had no answer. So I am still a little mystified about Bagdad.

Just before we reach Amboy we see the **Amboy Crater and Lava Field** to our right. This thing last erupted as recently as 500 years ago, and the lava can still be seen splattered around the area.

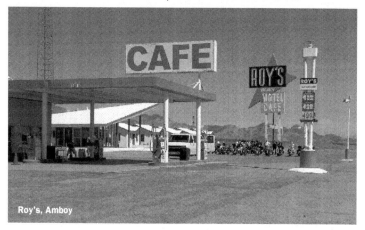
Roy's, Amboy

We stop at Roy's in Amboy to use the bathroom and stretch our legs. Roy's is a Route 66 icon, because it has been featured in several movies playing the part of the lone gas station in the desert. The café is long gone, although the guy working there did say it would be opening up again. Nothing else in this small town seems to be operating any more.

After leaving Amboy, watch out for the **Shoe Tree** on the right – yes, I did say shoe tree. It's not a tree shaped like a shoe but a tree with people's old shoes hanging all over it. A strange sight. Our giggles turned to laughter a bit further along the road when we came across a bra tree. Needless to say we spent the next 20 miles looking for a knickers tree, but we didn't see one! I suggested to Nuala that we plant the seed and start one but she wouldn't oblige. Perhaps it was too draughty with the air conditioning on in the truck!

Anyway enough of that, the next little town is **Essex**. Nothing much is happening here, so we press on. We cross over the I-40 and arrive in **Goffs**. There is a quaint railroad crossing here, so we wait for the next train to grab some pictures. Success - the driver sounded the horn, but it was probably because he was going over the crossing and not because some tourist was waving his arms at him.

Route 66 – Goff's Crossing

From here the hot dusty road takes us all the way to **Needles**, otherwise known as the 'Gateway to California'. Sitting on the scenic Colorado River recreation area, Needles is the hottest town in America and the home of Schultz, the creator of Charlie Brown. Keep your eyes open for the Schultz mural to the left as you drive through the town.

Crossing the border into Arizona, we have to hop on to the I-40 for a short way. Immediately after we cross the water we turn off back on to Route 66. The road is well signposted, which makes life easier, although my co driver is first class with a map. This part of Route 66 seems to be marked on the map as County Highway 10 for some reason.

Oatman, a small town in the Black Mountains of Arizona, is the next stop. This place is an old gold-mining town that dates back to the late 1800s. Oatman is an enjoyable place to visit, an old western town with dusty streets and wooden walkways down the side of the streets. The old buildings look original and there seems very little commercialism as the people go about their business at a slow pace.

Route 66 – Oatman mules

We were surprised when we parked up to be greeted by some wild burros (donkeys, to us Brits). These animals live wild in the surrounding hills, and every day they wander into the town to greet the tourists and look for food. They are very

86

tame, so we bought a bag of carrots for less than a dollar from one of the local shops and gave them an afternoon snack and a scratch behind the ear. They followed us to the shop and waited patiently at the doorway, which was very amusing.

At the weekends you can see a staged gunfight, but we passed through midweek so unfortunately didn't get to see the show.

Clark Gable loved this place and came here often to play poker. He also spent his honeymoon in the Oatman Hotel when he married Carol Lombard in 1939.

We really didn't want to leave, but after a quick beer and some country music at a bar we head off again towards **Kingman**. The road to Kingman is a scenic back-country drive. We have to navigate the seriously twisty and narrow road going down the Black Mountains past the old mining ruins of Gold Road. To our left we spot the wrecks of one or two cars which have gone over the edge in the past and are still there rusting away. At the foot of the mountains the road stretches out in front of us once again.

Mr D'z at Kingman

On the approach to Kingman we go under the I-40 and make a left. Route 66 takes us right into the town from here, and we stop at Mr D'z Route 66 Diner for some refreshment. The food here is basic but very good, and they serve breakfast all day, just what I need after a hard day in the leather seat. The staff are friendly and the whole place has a genuine Route 66 atmosphere. To top it off there are a couple of muscle cars and some Harley Davidsons in the car park.

A mile up the road we pull in for the night at a nice motel on the hill. The following morning we push on to **Peach Springs**. We pass several run-down old places that look as if they have been deserted for many years. Old cars and trucks are scattered around the landscape and there's the odd trailer in the middle of nowhere.

Peach Springs is said to be the inspiration for the fictional town of Radiator Springs in the Disney Pixar movie Cars. When the I-40 opened in 1978 this place and many other towns along Route 66 suffered from the loss of passing traffic. From here at Peach Springs there is a rough dirt road 72 miles long that leads all the way to the West Rim of the Grand Canyon and the famous Skywalk mentioned earlier. I would advise you to reach the West Rim by a different route as described earlier, unless you are feeling extra adventurous.

A few miles down the road we make a stop at the **Grand Canyon Caverns**. We had no idea what to expect here. At the very most we were expecting a few small connecting caves, but like everything in America, it is much bigger than you expect. We went down in the lift over 200 feet and emerged into what I can only describe as an underground cathedral. We had a tour of some connecting caverns which lasted around an hour. There are much longer tours that can be taken if you are a hardened cave explorer, but the short one was enough for us.

You have the option of spending the night down here too, as one of the caverns has been made into a hotel room with five-star service. Back up in the open air there is a camp site, RV park, convenience store and another inn for people who like to sleep above ground.

After turning in off Route 66, just follow the dirt road to your left. When you see the huge green dinosaur, you have arrived at the caverns.

Seligman is our next stop. This place takes you right back in time to the good old days of Route 66. The locals have done a great job of preserving the old-time look and keeping this place alive, with many shops, bars and restaurants still sporting the Route 66 theme. There are several motels and hotels to choose from, including the famous **Route 66 Motel** with its themed rooms. Be aware that if you stay here in Seligman for the night, you will hear the rumble of the Santa Fe trains throughout the night as they never stop, but it all adds to the experience.

From here Route 66 rolls on for a few miles towards Ash Fork before turning into the I-40. We headed off down to southern Arizona from here - you will need to make your own plans as to where you intend to go next. Back to Las Vegas perhaps, or Williams and the Grand Canyon are not far away, so maybe you want to head there.

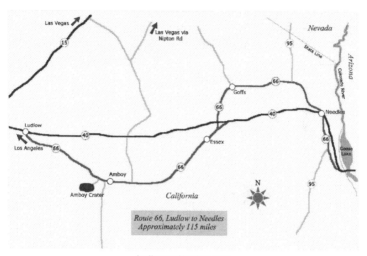

Ludlow to Needles map

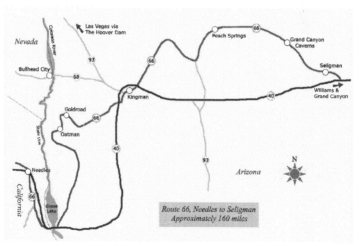

Needles to Seligman map

Primm
39 Miles

Primm, or Primm Valley as some people call it, can be found south of Las Vegas on the Nevada/California border. Primm is not a town but more of a cluster of casinos and gas stations with a shopping mall and huge rollercoaster thrown in.

If you like rollercoasters, then pay a visit to **Buffalo Bill's Casino and Hotel** here and ride the Desperado. When it was built in 1994 this 'coaster was the world's tallest, fastest and steepest. It is accessed from inside Buffalo Bill's Casino. The climb at the beginning seems to go on forever as your heart slowly comes up into your mouth and the hotel beneath you gets smaller. When you slowly tip over the top for the first drop you can't actually see where you're going, as it falls into a hole in the ground.

We like Buffalo Bill's Casino. We stayed in the hotel once when we were on our way south to drive along Route 66. The casino has a Wild West theme and the atmosphere is very relaxed, with many places to eat and a music bar with live entertainment. There is even a log flume water ride which floats you through the casino floor. If you stay at the hotel, check out the shape of the pool - a buffalo of course!

The **Fashion Outlets of Las Vegas** which I spoke about earlier in the shopping section can be found here, next to Primm Valley Resorts.

To get to Primm, just head south on the I-15 and you can't miss it. If you want a more interesting route, follow Las Vegas Boulevard (the Strip) south out of town until you come to a small place called **Jean**. Previously this old road would have taken us all the way to Primm. When you pass Jean the impression is that it still will, but we tried it last year and we had to double back after two or three miles as it came to a dead end, so jump on to the I-15 here at Jean and save yourself the trouble.

There's not much to be found here at Jean, only the Gold Strike hotel and casino and a small airport used mainly for sporting activities such as sky diving.

Mount Charleston
43 Miles

Mount Charleston is a popular destination for many reasons. It nestles in the Spring Mountains only 35 miles to the north west of Las Vegas. In the summer months when the Vegas valley is baking in very hot weather, a trip up the mountain where the temperature is much cooler, with mountain breezes and plenty of fresh air, can be a welcome escape.

12,000 feet at the highest point, Mount Charleston is surrounded by an abundance of natural beauty. Ponderosa pine and juniper trees hug the road on the drive to the top. Many wild animals inhabit this area, so keep your eyes peeled. Be careful of the wild desert tortoises which sometimes crawl out in to the road. Other wild animals that can be seen here are burros and deer.

There are some exceptional scenic hiking trails that will take you a million miles away from the desert floor below, 52 miles of them in total with scenic waterfalls and many wild flowers. We saw many picnic areas and camp sites for both tents and RV parking.

When you're at the top surrounded by peaks and breathtaking scenery, it's easy to forget that you are only a short distance away from the city of Las Vegas. We park up and treat ourselves to a drink at the bar, then sit outside in the sunshine relaxing and watching for wildlife.

If you wish to stay here overnight, the **Mount Charleston Resort** can be found at the top. If you like to ski or strap a snowboard to your feet then the **Las Vegas Ski and Snowboard Resort** is only a short drive away.

From the Strip, get on to the I-15 and head north. Take exit 42a on to the US-95 towards Reno. This will take you north out of the city, where you need to turn left on to Kyle Canyon Road. It is signposted Mount Charleston, so should be very easy to find. This road will take you all the way to the top.

Moab, Utah

Canyonlands National Park, Dead Horse Point State Park and Arches National Park all have the same pricing at $10 per vehicle or $5 per person on foot. This is for a 7-day pass.

460 Miles

Utah is our favourite state for sightseeing, famous for its unique red rock formations, natural arches and endless canyons. The state is an outdoor enthusiast's paradise, with an abundance of hiking trails, mountain biking, skiing and camping. Every road we drive along seems to have something interesting to look at or take a photo of.

Moab is on the east side of Utah, and has some of the most mind-blowing scenery we have ever seen. Here there are some of the best views of the Colorado River as it winds its way through endless canyons.

It's quite a long drive to get to Moab, so you may want to make it a three or four-day road trip and take in some sites along the way. It's around 460 miles from Las Vegas, but we think it's well worth it. If you like road trips, there are many distractions along the way and more than enough choice of places to stop off for the night.

The most interesting route for us to Moab is along Scenic Byway 12, but there are so many different and interesting routes across Utah with so many great sites to see that it's very hard to just recommend one.

Scenic byway 12

Head north out of Las Vegas on the I-15. We drive up as far as Cedar City and make a right turn to head east until we reached Panguitch. This is where Scenic Byway 12 starts.

Scenic Byway 12 has been designated an All-American Road. Only a small number of roads have achieved this status. Starting in the west at Panguitch, this road is roughly 125 miles long. Its snakes its way through red rock canyons, aspen forests, national parks and quaint little townships.

A route guide can be very useful, so pick one up in Panguitch or Bryce Canyon if you decide to stop there on your way. I will be talking about Bryce Canyon later. There will be a map of the area and all the places you will pass through on your way across Scenic Byway 12, with detailed information about each place.

You could spend forever sightseeing along this route. This is one of our favourite drives of all time, and we have cruised along it twice now from both directions. I could write a whole book about this road alone, and maybe I will. So if you're the type of person who likes to stop off at every vista you may want to add some time on to your trip.

You could easily spend the whole summer here in Utah travelling around seeing all the fabulous red rock formations and canyons, but still not get to see it all.

When you eventually arrive at Moab you will find plenty of motels and hotels to choose from. We prefer to use motels, as we like to have the truck close to hand - it makes loading and unloading the bags much easier. If you are like us and enjoy a good breakfast, then you will be pleased to see a Denny's at the north end of the town. The people in the visitor centre at Moab must have thought we were mad, because the first question we asked was if there was a Denny's in town. If you are not familiar with Denny's, take my word for it, they do great breakfasts.

Moab has many national parks scattered around. There are three main ones you don't want to miss. Remember too that nearly all national parks in the USA charge a fee to enter. Here it was $10 for each park and the pass is valid for seven days, so if you are spending more than one day in Moab you can always re-enter the park another day. And as I said earlier, you can also pay for a combined pass if you plan on visiting several national parks - this should save you some money. Check with the ranger at the kiosk when entering any of the parks, as they are very helpful and a good source of information.

The three parks of interest here in Moab are **Canyonlands National Park, The Arches National Park** and **Dead Horse State Park**. National Parks are created by Acts of Congress and administered by the US National Park Service, whereas state parks are the responsibility of the state. Dead Horse State Park is much smaller than the national parks but still requires an entry fee. This is where you will find Dead Horse Point, where they filmed the final scene of the movie Thelma and Louise, in which the women drive off the edge of a canyon.

Dead Horse Point

Looking out from Dead Horse Point was one of the highlights of our trip. You get a spectacular view of the Colorado River as it snakes its way through the canyon 2000 feet below, a scene which has taken the Colorado River millions of years to create.

On our visit we sat on the edge peering out for ages, not wanting to leave. You could almost be on the surface of Mars. It puts everything else into perspective and makes you realise how small and insignificant we really are.

Dead Horse Point is so called because back in the 1800s wild mustang herds were common in this area. Cowboys used this peninsula to corral and capture these wild horses behind a huge fence. The story goes that one time a herd of unwanted horses was left out here in the corral, where they died of thirst looking down upon the gushing Colorado river out of reach below. Looking down from the top of Dead Horse Point, we could see a dirt road snaking along a lower ledge beneath us. I wanted to find out where this road was coming from and going to. I also wanted to know if we could drive along it or was it just for the rangers' use. In fact you can - it's called the **Shafer Trail**. It can be accessed to the left just past the entry kiosk inside Canyonlands National Park. It is free to use, but we had to go to the visitor centre to get a pass from the rangers.

There's a choice of two routes on the Shafer Trail. We took the shortest, which snakes around Dead Horse Point and comes very close to the edge in some places. The road is flat and dusty. We were glad we had a four-wheel drive vehicle, although this trail can easily be driven in a two-wheel-drive car as long as the weather and the road are reasonably dry.

Most of the time we prefer a four-wheel-drive SUV anyway, because you are sitting higher up and get a slightly better view. Remember your rental car agreement may not allow you to venture off the main highway, so be sure to check.

Moab – Canyonlands National Park

The trail goes on for 17 miles through some barren-looking territory until we reach Potash, where the road turns into tarmac and eventually takes us back to Moab. It's easy to forget where you are when driving out here along this trail. In places there is a sheer towering rock face to your left, while to your right you see the Colorado River glistening far below. You get a powerful feeling of isolation out in the wilderness at times.

There is an abundance of campgrounds all over the place in and around the national parks, catering for people with tents and RVs. This is not for us as we like our home comforts too much. I keep threatening to rent an RV trailer one day to travel round America, just to see what it's like, but we haven't yet managed to get round to it.

Canyonlands National Park is huge, at over 500 square miles in extent, and you can spend all day here depending how adventurous you are. We spent an afternoon visiting all the viewing points (vistas) that are reachable by truck (when I say 'truck' I'm referring to the SUV or sports utility vehicle we always rent. If there is anywhere that specifically requires a truck or four-wheel-drive and is not accessible by car, I will always mention this).

There are many hiking trails that take you to fantastic vistas which you can't drive to. We don't mind a short hike now and again, but hiking for miles, for hours on end is not our thing unless we know for sure that there is something really spectacular to see when we get to the other end, so we mainly stick with the vehicle and short walks. We still get to see many awesome sights.

The **Arches National Park** is exactly what it says on the tin - a park full of red rock buttes and natural arches that have taken millions of years to form. Again there are many hiking trails, vistas and campgrounds, so have fun.

Monument Valley

Entrance fee to the Navajo Tribal Park is $5 per person
(scenic drive included)
400 Miles

Monument valley – view from Visitor Center

While in Moab, I suggest you make your trip a little longer and head down to the famous **Monument Valley** on the Arizona and Utah border. When you leave Arches, complete a big circle to end up back in Las Vegas. You have to get back to Vegas one way or another, and Monument Valley is the most scenic route you could imagine.

Monument Valley straddles the Arizona-Utah state line in the Navajo tribal park. Hundreds of millions of years ago this part of North America was an inland sea, but water and geological forces have transformed the valley into a collection of awe-inspiring buttes, canyons and pinnacles rising up from the desert floor.

A visit to this place is a thrilling experience. Every corner you turn and every hill you climb over unfolds some unique scenery that will stay in your memory forever. You will recognise this scenery from John

Wayne westerns such as *Stagecoach* and *The Searchers*, filmed here by John Ford.

We have visited this place on several occasions now. The first time was planned, but on subsequent occasions we visited on the way back from somewhere else, because when nearby we find Monument Valley irresistible - it reels us in every time.

This 2400-square mile area is the land of the Navajo nation, who still live and work here in the valley, making jewellery, weaving and farming animals. The traditional Navajo home is a mud covered house known as a Hogan. Many of the Navajo still live in these dwellings and they can be seen around the valley.

The US-163 is the scenic route that takes us straight through the centre of Monument Valley. It's a mouth-wide-open drive and one of the best scenic routes in North America. This road runs from Bluff in the north all the way down to Kayenta in the south.

Just south of a town called **Mexican Hat** (named after a butte nearby which resembles a Mexican sombrero) can be found one of the most photographed stretches of road in North America. You may recognise it from my picture.

Monument Valley road

This piece of road is easily recognisable if heading south and is pretty much the entrance to the Valley. The first time we came to Monument Valley we were heading north and completely missed this fantastic piece of scenery. The visitor centre is run by the Navajo and the view across the valley from here is spectacular. You will find a restaurant, gifts and guided tours here. There is a 17-mile scenic loop road that can be accessed from the visitor centre. This red, dusty road takes you out into the valley and up close to some of the most famous monuments.

Monument Valley - on the dirt road

We have driven this dirt road twice now and it was worth every minute, as it takes us beyond the highway and out into the depths of the valley, where it can be very quiet and totally natural. We felt as if we were in one of those old westerns and was expecting John Wayne to ride round the corner at any moment, although our V8 Jeep probably didn't fit into the scene too well.

Be warned though, this dirt road is like driving across a ploughed field and it's steep in places, so if you are worried about damaging your vehicle then take it very slow. There is no need for a four-wheel-drive - the road is suitable for most cars, just take care and you should be fine.

Alternatively take one of the guided tours that are operated from the visitor centre by the Navajo. They are not cheap, at around $75 for a two-hour trip, but you'll see a lot you would otherwise miss. The area has cliff dwellings, ancient caves and natural arches which are away from the scenic drive in more isolated areas and can only be seen on the guided tours.

Horses in Monument Valley

Wild horses can be seen grazing around the valley too. If you feel like jumping in the saddle and doing a John Wayne impression, there are one or two corrals where the Navajo will take you on a guided trek, for a fee of course.

The visitor centre can be found just off the US-163 at the crossroads almost in the centre of the valley. The opposite direction leads to **Goulding** and **Goulding Lodge**. This is a great experience if you want to stay overnight in the valley and see the sunset and rise over the red buttes, it really is a beautiful sight. Kayenta, Bluff and Mexican Hat also offer several places to stay overnight.

Las Vegas to Monument Valley is approximately 400 miles each way, so a three or even a four-day round trip would be advisable, taking in some other sights along the way.

I am not going to explain how to get to Monument Valley as the directions would become long and maybe confusing. Use that road map I suggested earlier.

Valley of the Gods, Utah
433 miles

The route you take to Monument Valley from Las Vegas will depend on which other places you intend to visit during your trip. I would recommend incorporating the **Valley of the Gods**, as it is only about 40 miles from Monument Valley, north on US-163. It is located on US-261 just north of Mexican Hat. We stumbled across it by mistake, but wow what a mistake!

We were driving east along the US-95 heading for Mexican Hat when we noticed on the map that the US-261 would be a shorter route, so we decided to turn on to it and chance our luck.

Just as we turned on to the US-261, we saw a sign that said this route became a dirt road 23 miles ahead. We had a four-wheel-drive Jeep, so we decided to go for it. As we were driving along this road we met the odd car and motorcycle coming in the opposite direction, which gave us plenty of confidence.

When we finally came to the dirt road mentioned on the sign we got a shock. We found ourselves over 6000 feet up at the top of Cedar Mesa, at a point known as **Mokee Dugway**, looking down across the Valley of the Gods in all its splendour. The valley was spread out for miles in front of us down below. With its red sandstone buttes and pinnacles on display, it was real geographical eye candy.

The dirt road the sign was referring to snakes its way down the side of the mountain to the bottom, where it turns back into tarmac and continues across the valley towards Mexican Hat. The road is very close to the edge and becomes quite steep in places, but I didn't get where I am today by being a pussy, so we went down head first.

There's another dirt road to the right at the top which leads to **Mulie Point**, about two miles over. Take care at Mulie Point, as it is very close to the edge with no barrier.

These dirt roads are easily accessible for small cars and bikes and we saw several Harley Davidsons on their way up as we were going down, but I wouldn't advise this route for an RV unless you are very brave. The smaller RVs would probably be able to get up and down the twisty dirt road, but I wouldn't advise trying it with a big one. The dirt road down the side of the mountain is just wider than a car, so you have to pull over if you meet someone coming the other way.

Valley of the Gods – view from Mokee Dugway

My photo shows the view from the top of the Mesa at Mokee Dugway. Part of the dirt road can be seen snaking its way down. A scenic drive can be seen going left off the US-261 in the distance.

After lots of nervous shouting, with my passenger gripping tightly on to the seat, we reached the bottom of the dirt road down Cedar Mesa safely. Now there are two choices. The tarmac US-261 takes you towards Mexican Hat, while the red dusty road to the left called Valley of the Gods Road will take you on a 16-mile scenic drive around the Valley to view some of the buttes and pinnacles up close. So this is a no-brainer for us.

The scenic drive comes out on the US-163 a few miles north of Mexican Hat, so we didn't have to double back. The Valley of the Gods is comparable to Monument Valley, and we decided it ought to be called Monument Valley Two. There are not many tourists here, no tour buses and no visitor centre. You can see the vast desert plain stretching out for miles, with towering red sandstone buttes and pinnacles. We pulled over to the side and wore out the batteries in our cameras trying to photograph it all. But you can never completely capture sights like this - you have to experience them for real. No wonder this place is known as a photographer's paradise!

With so few tourists here this place is quiet and peaceful and the whole experience is very natural. If you stop to enjoy the view, remember you are in the middle of a desert, so if you start poking around in the brush and walking too far away from your vehicle you must watch out for rattlesnakes. If you hear a rattle, turn and walk in the other direction. Now! If you intend to come here after visiting Monument Valley, you will be going in the opposite direction to the one we took. This is no problem, you certainly won't be missing anything. I suggest that after leaving Monument Valley heading north on the US-163, instead of turning left on to the US-261 just north of Mexican Hat, carry on for 2-3 miles and just after Nipple Rock (its actually called Flag Butte but you will know exactly where I mean by Nipple Rock) there is a dirt road to the left. This is the scenic route around the Valley of the Gods, and it will bring you out on the US-261 close to the bottom of Cedar Mesa.

Hole n' the Rock, Utah
Home tour $5 per person, children under 5 free

We were driving along Highway 191 on the east side of Utah en route to Moab, admiring the red rock formations and natural arches, when purely by accident we stumbled across one of the strangest places we have ever seen. At first all we could see was a huge red rock with 'Hole n' the Rock' written across it in huge white letters. When we stopped we found a huge house had been carved out of the rock, covering some 5000 square feet with 14 rooms.

This man-made engineering marvel was cut out of the rock in the 1940s by a guy named Albert Christensen, who lived here with his wife Gladys. Albert drilled and blasted away at the rock for twelve years until he was finally able to move in with his wife in 1952. He continued to carve out the rock and make the dwelling larger even after moving in. He also had plans to build a balcony for Gladys, but died before he could complete it.

In the 1950s Albert and Gladys ran a roadside diner here and people would come from miles away to sample the best steaks in the desert. Nowadays the diner is a gift shop. If you want to see the rest of the dwelling where Albert and Gladys lived, this is where the tour starts from.

As we were already in the gift shop we decided to take the tour, which was well worth the money. The place is huge, and it's hard to believe it was all carved by one man over a period of twenty years. We learned all about the story of their journey on this planet and what determined and business-minded people they were. We were not allowed to take any pictures of the inside of the house while on the tour, which is understandable.

When Albert wasn't hammering at the rock he liked taxidermy, so expect to find several stuffed animals around the house, including horses and a donkey named Harry, apparently the most famous dead donkey in the south west. All very interesting, though personally stuffed animals give me the creeps.

Sadly Albert died in 1957. Gladys kept running the diner until she died in 1974. They are both laid to rest in a small alcove not far from the entrance to the shop. Outside there is a trading post, along with a zoo and lots of old mining memorabilia scattered around.

Bryce Canyon, Utah

Park entrance fee $20 per vehicle, $10 per motorcycle, bicycle or on foot, pass valid for 7 days.

254 Miles

Scenic Byway 12 – Red Rock Tunnel

En route to Bryce Canyon we drive along Scenic Byway 12 through Utah. The road drifts in and out of the Dixie National Forest, and along this scenic route are some of the most spectacular rock formations we have ever seen while driving.

The picture on the previous page shows the tunnel in the rock, which I took in June 2010, it is one of my favourite snaps. There are many photo opportunities along this road, so be sure to carry some spare batteries for your camera or you may end up disappointed.

Bryce Canyon – hiking trails

Bryce Canyon is not actually a canyon but a series of amphitheatres on the edge of the Paunsaugunt Plateau in southern Utah. This national park has 18 miles of paved roads and over 50 miles of hiking trails meandering through some extraordinary rock formations called hoodoos. The hoodoos, created by erosion, look like stalagmites or upside-down icicles. Their stunning pinks, reds, oranges and golden browns change every moment from sunrise to sunset. For the artist or photographer these beautiful rock formations that nature took millions of years to create are a must-see. Some trails lead down through the hoodoos, where we encountered stunning overlooks and scenic wonders. Bryce Canyon is a magical and spell-binding place as you look over the hills and see the formations of hoodoos with the spruce, fir and aspen trees growing between their spires. On a clear day you can see for more than 100 miles, and at certain times of the year at Rainbow Point and Yovimpa Point it is so clear that your view is limited only by the curvature of the Earth.

As we drive deeper into the park we climb another 1200 feet. At the highest point we reach 9100 feet above sea level.

We pop into the visitor centre and grab a free local map. It is worth having a look at the exhibits, publications and free 22 minute video about this canyon, showing us where the best viewing areas are and what there is to see along the paved trails.

Camping and lodging are available if you wish to stay overnight in the canyon and spend a few days exploring further. Bryce Canyon Lodge was built in the early 1920s with local timbers and stone, and accurately reflects the rustic flavour of the period. The lodge has a restaurant, gift shop and post office where you can take this opportunity to send a postcard or two, while sipping a cup of tea and maybe even a slice of coconut cream pie.

For nature lovers, the canyon is full of wildlife and wild flowers. We saw chipmunks, lizards and a family of deer on the way down the trail, grazing openly on the grass in front of us. Please watch out for the deer when driving in the park, as they can run out in front of your vehicle at any time. Use caution at all times to preserve the wildlife of this area, as well as the front of your car.

Rainbow Point is at the far end of the park. On a clear day here you can see far beyond the Navajo Mountains to the Kaibab Plateau (the north rim of the Grand Canyon) in Arizona, some 90 miles away, with New Mexico even further in the distance. The foreground views of the hoodoos and long-eroded slopes are awash with stunning hues of reds, pinks and golden browns, all mixed in with the greenery of the pine trees.

Poodle Rock, Bryce Canyon

If you look hard enough at Rainbow Point you will see a poodle-shaped rock. It is not easy to find, even though it is right in front of you. We enlisted the help of some fellow eagle-eyed tourists to help us track it down, but it still took us about fifteen minutes to spot it. To see it you need to be standing in the right place, but you also need to be looking at the correct angle, otherwise it will look much like any other rock nearby. A small clue - the pink cliffs make a stunning backdrop behind the poodle.

Bryce canyon – hoodoos at the Amphitheatre

Many hiking trails start and end at Rainbow Point. We took a trek down to meander among the hoodoos and the pink cliffs. There is a pleasant picnic area down among the pink and white rocks, where several people had gathered to take in the beauty of the place. On the way back towards the entrance of the park we stop to see the **Natural Bridge**, which was formed by rain and frost erosion. Almost back at the entrance to the park we encounter the **Bryce Amphitheatre**. This was the highlight of the park for us, with the most spectacular panoramic views encompassing the Black Mountain range to the north east and the Navajo Mountains in the south. The colours and hues we saw here are indelibly etched in our memories, as well as in the camera. This is the best place to capture the changing light formations on the hoodoos, cliff formations and plateaus from sunrise to sunset in the park.

Montezuma Castle
302 Miles

In the heart of Arizona, in the Verde Valley, is a cliff-dwelling the like of which we had never seen before. High up on the side of the cliff face is a 20-room castle carved out of limestone. The Montezuma Castle was built by the Sinagua people over a thousand years ago and there is an interesting story behind it.

109

The Sinagua people must have been very clever to have built this castle so high up the cliff face. They would have had to use ladders to get in and out of the castle as the access is almost vertical, so imagine how difficult it must have been carving this place out of the rock so high up.

The castle gave these people protection from other tribes who threatened their way of life. Its location high up in the rock face would have given them a great view out across the land and provided advance warning of anyone approaching, thus making it easier to defend.

The castle is south facing, taking in the sun's rays in the summer months and offering some protection from cold winds, rain and snow during the winter. The castle's name was a mistake. It was believed that Montezuma, an Aztec Emperor, resided here, but in fact Montezuma never strayed from his home in New Mexico. The people who lived here were farmers who tended the land below and used the river to survive.

I wish we had come here a few years earlier, when the castle was still open to tourists. I would have loved to climb the ladders to see inside, but for preservation reasons the building is now closed and can only be admired from below.

On the ground level there are some more ruins believed to be of the kitchen area, where bread and other foods were prepared.

While walking around the meandering woodland pathways below, we felt as if we had stepped back in time, and got a sense of how these people lived all those years ago. We sat and watched chipmunks playing on the rock face beneath the castle. I was also mesmerised by a woodpecker boring a hole into the tree next to me.

Montezuma Castle is right next to the I-17 near the small town of Camp Verde. To get here the easiest route would be along the I-40 from Kingman and then on to the I-17 at Flagstaff and south. But we prefer the smaller more scenic roads, as you know by now, so we turned off the I-40 at Ash Fork on to the US-89 and headed down towards Paulden, then through the expanse of the awesome Chino Valley. At Yavapai we took a left on to the US-89a and headed towards **Jerome**.

Jerome is a tiny town built high up on the side of the mountain. This old historic town is astonishing in the way it has been built, with houses looking as if they are balanced on the edge. The roads through the town were spectacular to drive, with awesomely beautiful views.

At the town of Cottonwood we pick up the US-260 and head for Camp Verde, where we check in at the **Territorial Inn** for the night. This is a great little motel with some stunning hand made furniture built from juniper logs that Nuala instantly fell in love with. I was able to haggle the price down with a friendly lady behind reception - just the job.

We visited Montezuma Castle first thing in the morning and decided to head back to Las Vegas through the town of **Sedona**. We crossed over the I-17 on to the US-179, a stunning drive that took us all the way there.

The Sedona area is well known for its red and golden-brown rock formations, which stretch out for mile after mile. The thick woodland has some of the biggest pine trees we had ever seen. Some people say the drive through the Sedona region is the best scenic route in North America. I agree it's a candidate, but for me the jury is still out as to whether it's the best.

Four Corners Monument
Entrance fee $3 per person, all ages
454 Miles

The Four Corners Monument on the US-160 highway is the only place in America where the corners of four states meet in one place. Here, by getting down on your hands and knees, you can have one limb each in Arizona, Utah, Colorado and New Mexico. A huge bronze disk was placed here after some refurbishment of the area in 1992, but the original marker point has been here since 1912. We found some native Americans selling jewellery and crafts, but there is not much else here – it was a quick photo opportunity and away. We arrived here late, ten minutes before they were due to close, so we didn't have to pay. There is not much to see nearby, as the area is fairly desolate. The nearest place we could find to bed down for the night was Cortez, about 40 miles away in Colorado.

I have mentioned this place here because if you are visiting Monument Valley, Four Corners Monument is not too far away.

At the Four Corners Monument

HANDY WEBSITES

The following four websites are a great source of information and rooms

i4vegas.com
Great deals on hotel rooms and details of resort fees

Vegas.com
Good for hotel rooms and a great source of information about what's happening in Vegas

Vegasview.com
Good deals on hotel rooms and lots more information

LVTB.com
Very few hotel rooms but some other useful information
(Las Vegas Tourist Bureau)

Airlines own websites that fly to the USA from UK

Virgin-Atlantic.com - Direct flights only

USAirways.com/uk - Indirect flights – one or more stops

BritishAirways.com - Direct and indirect flights

AmericanAirlines.co.uk - Direct and indirect flights

Delta.com - Indirect flights – one or more stops

United.com - Indirect flights – one or more stops

Aircanada.com/uk - Indirect flights – one or more stops

Lufthansa.com/uk - Indirect flights – one or more stops

Theses websites are known as 'screen scrapers' and search the internet to deliver the best prices

Flights

Dialaflight.com
A good search facility for flights, hotels and car rental but can't be booked online – 0844 811 4444

Cheapflights.co.uk
Some cheap flights to be found here, but you will need to be very flexible with your dates.

Fly24.co.uk - Flights only

Car Rental

Arguscarhire.com
Rentalcars.com (Previously known as Carhire3000.com)

Flights, hotels and car rental

Netflights.co.uk
Expedia.co.uk
Opodo.co.uk
ebookers.com
Travelsupermarket.com
Lastminute.com
Kayak.co.uk
Goamerica.co.uk
Dealchecker.co.uk
Holidaygenie.com
Travelbag.co.uk
Skyscanner.net

2074865R00068

Printed in Great Britain
by Amazon.co.uk, Ltd.,
Marston Gate.